Lord and Christ

Lord and Christ

The Implications of Lordship for Faith and Life

For to this end Christ died and rose and lived again,
that He might be Lord of both the dead and the living.
—Romans 14:9

Therefore let all the house of Israel know assuredly
that God has made this Jesus, whom you crucified,
both Lord and Christ.
—Acts 2:36

Ernest C. Reisinger

P U B L I S H I N G
P.O. BOX 817 • PHILLIPSBURG • NEW JERSEY 08865

Unless otherwise indicated, Scripture quotations are from The Holy Bible, New King James Version. Copyright © 1979, 1980, 1982, Thomas Nelson, Inc. Italics indicates emphasis added.

Printed in the United States of America

Library of Congress Cataloging-in-Publication Data

Reisinger, Ernest C., 1919—
    Lord and Christ : the implications of Lordship for faith and life / Ernest C. Reisinger.
       p. cm.
    Includes bibliographical references.
    ISBN 0-87552-388-9
    1. Salvation. 2. Jesus Christ—Lordship. 3. Evangelicalism. I. Title.
BT752.R45 1994
232—dc20   94–33274

ACKNOWLEDGMENTS
AND
THANKS

TO

*The wife of my youth
without whose assistance and patience
this book would not exist;*

AND

*Robert G. den Dulk,
past president of
Westminster Theological Seminary in California
for his encouragement and helpful suggestions;*

AND

*James Eshelman,
manager of Banner of Truth Trust, USA,
for his reading the manuscript.*

Contents

Foreword

A physician is no better than his diagnostic skills. If he fails to make an accurate analysis of the presenting problem, serious underlying causes may go undetected. Misdiagnosis impedes healing and may even promote death. The patient who is mistakenly told that his malignant tumor is benign may feel relieved, but he is in grave danger. He will not know how sick he is, and consequently will feel no impulse to take corrective measures, until he receives an accurate report.

Diagnosis is equally critical in the spiritual world. Failure to assess accurately the issues and problems that confront the Christian church inevitably stifles spiritual growth and fosters superficiality. That was the reason for God's complaint against Judah's leaders during Jeremiah's ministry. The Lord held the prophets and priests responsible, charging, "They have also healed the hurt of My people slightly, saying, 'Peace, peace!' when there is no peace" (Jer. 6:14). Simplistic assessments lead to insufficient treatments.

One of the most challenging issues facing American evangelicals today is the so-called "lordship controversy." The popularization of the idea that a person may be converted by receiving Jesus Christ as Savior and not as Lord has created a tremendous debate among Bible-believing Christians. Charges and countercharges have been exchanged between the lordship and nonlordship camps. Arguments from both sides have been repeatedly examined and answered in numerous articles, books, and conferences. Too often the debate has generated more heat than light.

In this book Ernest C. Reisinger enters the debate decidedly on the side of the "lordship teachers." Yet, he writes not as a cheerleader interested in adding to the crowd noise but as an analyst promoting understanding of the conflict. Like a master diagnostician, Reisinger subjects the whole controversy to an incriminating doctrinal examination.

Taken from a series of articles that initially appeared in the *Founders Journal*, the analysis that follows serves as a theological CAT scan of the nonlordship position, revealing inconspicuous yet pernicious errors that lie beneath the surface of the debate. What does this position say about repentance, faith, regeneration, justification, and sanctification? Reisinger carefully demonstrates that these and other biblical doctrines are disfigured beyond recognition where the nonlordship view is allowed to flourish.

While not every nonlordship *adherent* is guilty of distorting all these crucial doctrines, all nonlordship *teaching* inevitably is. Many believers are happily inconsistent in their unwillingness to own the necessary implications and consequences of their views. It is conceivable that some may not actually see the implications that the nonlordship perspective has for the fundamental doctrines of the gospel message. A careful reading of this book will dispel such ignorance.

Ernest Reisinger forces us to recognize that ideas have consequences. And the inescapable consequence of nonlordship teaching is ultimately the loss of the gospel itself. This diagnosis is not pleasant to consider, but it is essential to the recovery and maintenance of a vibrant, biblical Christianity. Without a clear understanding of the problem, there will be no adequate prescription of a cure.

After exposing the theological fallacies of nonlordship arguments, this book points us back to the purer, life-giving stream of historic Christian orthodoxy. Reisinger commends the old gospel: that gospel which was known and preached by the great soul winner Charles Spurgeon, by those great instruments of revival Jonathan Edwards and George White-field, by the seventeenth-century theological giants known as Puritans, and by those fearless Reformers Martin Luther, John Calvin, and John Knox. This book unashamedly contends for the gospel as it is expounded in the Westminster Confession of Faith, the Second London Baptist Confession of Faith, and the Heidelberg Catechism.

Make no mistake, it is the nonlordship proponents who have deviated from the biblical teachings on salvation. With theological precision, pastoral sensitivity, and reformational passion, Ernest Reisinger exposes their errors and charts the course back to "the old paths, where the good way is."

Martin Luther said:

> If I profess with the loudest voice and clearest exposition every portion of the truth of God except precisely that little point which the world and the devil are at that moment attacking, I am not confessing Christ, however boldly I may be professing Christ. Where the battle rages, there the loyalty of the soldier is proved, and to be steady on all the battle-fields besides, is merely flight and disgrace if he flinches at that point.

Written by one who has been in the battle for over forty years, this book should not be regarded as simply more fuel for the fires of controversy. Rather, it represents a loyal soldier's faithful confession of Jesus Christ. It honorably defends and proclaims Him whom the angel announced, the one and only Savior, who is Lord and Christ.

THOMAS K. ASCOL

Preface

The purpose of this volume is not to duplicate some excellent books that have already been published, such as *Lord of the Saved*, by Kenneth L. Gentry, Jr., *Christ the Lord*, edited by Michael S. Horton, and *A Layman's Guide to the Lordship Controversy*, by Richard P. Belcher. I heartily recommend all three of these, among others.

I have carefully read books by the leading opponents of lordship salvation, including three respected teachers, Zane C. Hodges, Charles C. Ryrie, and Robert P. Lightner. My intention is not to attack them personally. Rather it is to address some very important theological differences and show that nonlordship teachings fall outside the historical stream of theology expressed in the long-respected and tested creeds and confessions, such as, the Heidelberg Catechism, the Westminster Confession of Faith, the London Confession of 1689, and the *Institutes of the Christian Religion*.

There were two principal catalysts to my writing this book. The first was Charles Ryrie's statement in *Balancing the Christian Life* (Chicago: Moody, 1969), referring to lordship preachers (p. 170):

> The importance of this question cannot be overestimated in relation to both salvation and sanctification.

The message of faith only and the message of faith plus commitment of life cannot both be the gospel; therefore, one of them is false and comes under the curse of perverting the gospel or preaching another gospel.

The second catalyst was the terrible reaction of many nonlordship teachers and writers to John MacArthur's book *The Gospel According to Jesus,* which was often subjected to misrepresentation or misunderstanding, or both.

The lordship debate did not begin with MacArthur's book. The nonlordship view can be traced to many notes in the Scofield Bible. This antinomian ("anti-law") teaching received earlier expression in the Marrow Controversy and in Sandemanianism of the eighteenth century. James I. Packer explains the connection between the current nonlordship view of saving faith and Sandemanianism in an article entitled "History Repeats Itself," published in *Christianity Today* ([Sept. 22, 1989], 22).

> The view that saving faith is no more than "belief of the truth about Christ's atoning death" is not new. It was put forward in the mid-eighteenth century by the Scot Robert Sandeman.
>
> Sandeman was the son-in-law to John Glas, founder of a denomination (now extinct) that practiced foot washing, love feasts, holy kissing, sharing of wealth, and choice of ministers from among the theologically uneducated—all in direct imitation of the New Testament church. A combative man proselytizing for this new body, Sandeman attacked the experimental religion of the Evangelical Revival. In his *Letters on Theron and Aspasio (Theron and Aspasio* was a popular book presenting revival piety), Sandeman affirmed that "every one who . . . is persuaded that the event (i.e., Christ's atoning death) actually happened as testified by the Apostles is justified."

No exercise of the affections in choice, or of the will in repentance, belongs to faith as such. From this position Sandeman accused leaders such as White-field and Wesley of destructive legalism for teaching that justifying faith includes desire for a new life through Christ, and for saying that without this desire there is no true faith and thus no salvation. His avowed motive was only to keep pure the doctrine of justification by faith, which to his mind the evangelical leaders were obscuring.

As warrant for his intellectualist idea of faith, Sandeman relied mainly on two passages in the New Testament. He took Romans 4:5, which speaks of "believing on him who justifies the ungodly," as showing that a believer is actually ungodly, because impenitent at the moment of his or her first believing. He took 1 John 5:1, which says that "Whosoever believes that Jesus is the Christ is born of God," as showing that regeneration follows assent to orthodoxy about Jesus' saving work.

Evangelical leaders William Williams, the great Welsh hymn writer; Andrew Fuller, William Carey's chief supporter; and Thomas Scott, the Anglican Bible commentator, all wrote against Sandeman's views. They argued that he was misinterpreting his two texts and ignoring many New Testament passages that depict faith as an exercise of the heart, involving a penitent purpose of living henceforth for God. They urged that the effect of Sandemanian belief would be at least, in Williams's phrase, "believing without power, making little of conviction and of a broken heart," and at worst would be the self-deception of believing that one was a believer when one was not.

The great Welsh preacher, Christmas Evans, testified a century later that the Sandemanianism that he temporarily embraced led him into cold-hearted ministry, passionate in enforcing orthodoxy but perfunctory in evangelism. "The Sandemanianism heresy affected me so far as to quench the spirit of prayer for the conversion of sinners, and it induced in my mind a greater regard for the smaller things of the Kingdom of Heaven than for the greater. I lost the strength which clothed my mind with zeal, confidence, and earnestness in the pulpit for the conversion of souls to Christ."

The narrow intellectualism of Sandeman's view of faith dampened life-changing evangelism. This was one reason why the Glasite-Sandemanian denomination did not survive.

From this we see that the lordship controversy is not new—it is just an old error with a new dress. For example, in his book *The Gospel Under Siege* (Dallas: Redencion Viva, 1981), Zane Hodges writes that "much evangelical gospel preaching is guilty of compromising the grace of the gospel." He insists that "there is no necessary connection between saving faith and works. In fact, to insist on good works as an evidence of salvation introduces obedience into the plan of salvation, compromising seriously, if not fatally, the freeness of the gospel offer."

Contrasting Theologies

Hodges rightly notes that "the Lordship Salvation debate is a debate over the gospel and, specifically, the nature of salvation, saving faith, and the relation of salvation to sanctification." Indeed, behind this one controversy lies a wide range of the theological differences between the nonlordship and lordship teachings on the foundational doctrines of the Christian faith. It is no exaggeration to say that these two positions represent two starkly contrasting theologies. This book will examine a number of crucial theological differences between the nonlordship and the lordship views.

It is not uncommon to hear people say, "Don't talk theology to me, just tell me about Jesus." Though that may sound very pious, the truth is that whenever we teach who Jesus is, what He did, and why He did it—His virgin birth, His sinless life, His vicarious suffering, His victorious resurrection—we engage in the deepest kind of theology.

Every Christian has a theology whether he knows it by that name or not. "Theology" is a compound of two words basically meaning an account of, or discourse about, gods or God. The word denotes teaching about God and His relationship to the world from Creation to the Consummation. The acid test of true theology was well expressed (if not always exemplified) by Thomas Aquinas: "Theology is taught by God, teaches of God, and leads to God."

Charles Hodge, speaking of the necessity of systematic theology, wrote (in his *Systematic Theology*, 3 vols. [Grand Rapids: Eerdmans, 1952], 1:2):

> It may naturally be asked, why not take the truths as God has seen fit to reveal them, and thus save ourselves the trouble of showing their relation and harmony? The answer to this question is, in the first place, that it cannot be done. Such is the constitution of the human mind that it cannot help endeavoring to systematize and reconcile the facts which it admits to be true. In no department of knowledge have men been satisfied with the possession of a mass of undigested facts. And the students of the Bible can as little be expected to be thus satisfied. There is a necessity, therefore, for the construction of systems of theology. Of this the history of the Church affords abundant proof. In all ages and among all denominations, such systems have been produced. It cost the Church centuries of study and controversy to solve the problems concerning the person of Christ; that is, to adjust and bring into harmonious arrangement all the facts which the Bible teaches on that subject. We have no choice in this matter. If we would discharge our duty as teachers and defenders of the truth, we

must endeavor to bring all the facts of revelation into systematic order and mutual relationship.

As we shall see, one of the chief errors of the nonlordship teaching is that it sets up an antithesis between biblical truths that are meant to exist in harmony with each other, such as saving faith and works, law and gospel, and law and grace.

On one very important point the nonlordship and lordship teachers agree: what is at stake is the very nature of the gospel. But the question is, Which position represents the true gospel?

Below are excerpts from four of the most respected and able theologians, authors, teachers, and preachers among the nonlordship family. Bear in mind that the views held by these men are exceedingly popular in American evangelicalism today.

One excerpt quoted earlier from Charles C. Ryrie's *Balancing the Christian Life* (p. 170) bears repeating here:

> The importance of this question cannot be overestimated in relation to both salvation and sanctification. The message of faith only and the message of faith plus commitment of life cannot both be the gospel; therefore, one of them is false and comes under the curse of perverting the gospel or preaching another gospel.

Likewise, Robert P. Lightner, in *The Savior, Sin, and Salvation* (Nashville: Nelson, 1991), writes: "These views—the absolutely free gift view and the Lordship view—cannot both be right. They are mutually exclusive" (p. 200). Both Ryrie and Lightner are correct in assessing the serious difference between the two views.

A statement by Lewis S. Chafer in *Grace: The Glorious Theme* (Grand Rapids: Zondervan, 1922, 1950) goes a step further, showing with amazing candor the side effects of the nonlordship view: "The Christian's liberty *to do precisely as he chooses* is as limitless and perfect as any other aspect of grace" (p. 345).

Zane C. Hodges, in *The Gospel Under Seige,* adds: "Saving faith is taking God at His Word in the gospel. It is nothing less than this. But it is also nothing more." Regarding God's loving call to salvation, Hodges writes, "God's love can embrace sinful people unconditionally, with no binding requirements attached at all." Salvation, he argues, involves "no spiritual commitment whatsoever" (p. 14).

If the statements by these four spokesmen are biblically true, then most of the content of this book is false and dangerous. All agree that both views cannot be correct. The differences are indeed great—so great, in fact, that the nonlordship gospel summarized under titles such as Hodges's *Absolutely Free!* could, for many, prove eternally costly.

ONE

Behind the
Lordship Controversy

One old Puritan said that the dangers in controversy are greater than the dangers of women and wine. I do not know if this is true or not, but I do know every true Christian loathes needless controversy, and all the more when it is among the family of God. Yet we must not forget that most, if not all, the great creeds and confessions of the church were born out of religious controversy.

In his recent book *Wrongly Dividing the Word of Truth*, John H. Gerstner says, "When the book *The Gospel According to Jesus* by John MacArthur appeared, the fat was in the fire." It was MacArthur's book that brought the "lordship controversy" to full flame. *The Gospel According to Jesus* has provoked pamphlets, books, sermons, seminars, conferences, and more. Three books that stand out in the controversy were written by champions of the dispensational school of theology: *So Great Salvation* by Charles C. Ryrie, *Absolutely Free!* by Zane C. Hodges, and *Sin, the Savior, and Salvation* by Robert P. Lightner.

What is behind the lordship controversy? The answer is *conflicting theologies*. And one reason I am happy to see this particular controversy is that it is bringing some theological

1

skeletons out of the closet. As writers debate in print the issues concerning lordship, they reveal their underlying theological commitments. It becomes clear that nonlordship advocates stand outside the biblical mainstream of theology
historically believed by the Reformers and the great teachers
in the church. And we are left to wonder how much regard
popular theologians today have for the great creeds and confessions of the faith.

No body of believers is immune to corruption in doctrine and practice. If examined by the great Head of the
church, each one would have some just charge against it. And
yet, while the apostle Paul earnestly resisted error wherever
he found it, he did not castigate those who built on the right
foundation. Despite impurities among them that would ultimately be consumed, he did not treat them as enemies *if their
foundation was Christ the Lord.* Even Paul's conduct toward the
enemies of our Lord did not seek to turn upon them the con-
tempt of all mankind. Rather, his treatment of them was cal-
culated for their good. I pray that such may be my motiva-
tion as well.

A Family of Doctrines

The lordship controversy will never be solved as an isolated
problem. It is inseparably connected to a theological system.
The various teachings of that system cannot be divided from
each other, despite its emphasis on "rightly divide the word
of truth."

As a child is part of a family, with a father and mother
and brothers and sisters and possibly cousins, the lordship
and nonlordship positions have family ties with other doctrines as well.

The father of nonlordship is called Arminianism. The
mother is dispensationalism (her sister being antinomianism). As the offspring of Arminianism and dispensationalism, the nonlordship view is fully related to and influenced
by them. So also are the siblings of nonlordship, which ex-

plains the strong family resemblances between so many doctrines. In other words, the lordship controversy is not an orphan standing by itself. It is closely related to many other doctrines. Each of the following topics shares the distinctive family traits of one or the other position:

1. Who Jesus really is and where He is
2. The nature of saving faith
3. Regeneration
4. Repentance
5. Justification
6. Sanctification
7. The inseparable relationship between justification and sanctification
8. The biblical doctrine of assurance
9. The condition of man
10. The character of God (sovereign in creation, sovereign in redemption, and sovereign in providence)
11. The relationship of the Ten Commandments to evangelism and to the Christian life

I will address several of these doctrines as they are influenced by their "father" and "mother," particularly the theological system of dispensationalism.

To demonstrate the influence of dispensationalism on the question of Christ's lordship, consider the following passages of Scripture. Would these texts not put to rest the lordship controversy if it were not tied to the whole system of dispensationalism theology?

- At our Lord's birth the angels announced Him as *Lord*. "For there is born to you this day in the city of David a Savior, who is Christ the Lord" (Luke 2:11). His saviorhood is within His lordship, not apart from it.
- The New Testament preachers spoke of Him as *Lord*. "For we do not preach ourselves, but Christ Jesus the Lord" (2 Cor. 4:5).

- In the Book of Acts, the sacred manual of evangelism, the word "Savior" occurs only twice, "Lord" 92 times, the phrase "Lord Jesus Christ" 6 times, and "Lord Jesus" 13 times. This should tell us something about the apostles' evangelism.
- In the New Testament, sinners received Jesus as *Lord*. "As you have therefore received Christ Jesus the Lord, so walk in Him" (Col. 2:6).
- The dying thief recognized that Jesus was *Lord*. "Lord, remember me . . ." (Luke 23:42).
- The adulterous woman in John 8 knew who Jesus was. When He asked her, "Where are those accusers of yours? Has no one condemned you?" she answered, "No one, Lord" (vv. 10–11).
- When the doubting Thomas realized who Jesus was in John 20:28, he exclaimed, "My Lord and my God!"
- Jesus Himself affirmed this truth in John 13:13: "You call me Teacher and Lord, and you say well, for so I am."
- The first apostolic sermon should settle the question, in which Peter declared, "Therefore let all the house of Israel know assuredly that God has made this Jesus, whom you crucified, both Lord and Christ" (Acts 2:36).
- Paul tells us that the very reason that Jesus died and rose again is that He might be *Lord*. "For to this end Christ died and rose and lived again, that He might be Lord of both the dead and living" (Rom. 14:9).
- In Philippians 2:5–8 the great apostle gives us the steps of our Lord's humiliation, and then in verses 9–11 he speaks of His exaltation. We are assured in these passages that all men will bow the knee, and that every tongue will confess. Confess what? "That Jesus Christ is Lord, to the glory of God the Father." Notice the words "every knee" and "every tongue"— some in restitution but all in recognition.

In the light of the above Scriptures, which trace Jesus' life from the cradle to the cross, the resurrection, and the heavenly throne, how could there even be a question about His lordship, let alone a controversy?

Serious Implications

It is a great comfort for Christians to know that Christ is Lord regardless of what men say or think. Further, it is a comfort to know that we have placed our hand in that sovereign, nail-pierced hand to lead us through sorrow, sickness, and death. If you are a believer but have not yet experienced these things, be patient; you will.

Consider some of the serious implications of Jesus' lordship:

1. Lordship implies our entire submission from the outset. It is a strange salvation that knows nothing about daily submission to Christ the Lord.

2. Lordship implies our willing service. The most outstanding conversion in the history of the church was that of the apostle Paul, recorded in Acts 9. It is interesting to note two questions Paul asked in verses 5 and 6: "Who are you, Lord?" and "What do You want me to do?" These are questions of a willing servant.

3. Lordship implies obedience. Jesus said in Luke 6:46, "Why do you call Me 'Lord, Lord,' and do not do the things which I say?"

4. Lordship implies ownership. If Jesus is my Lord, He owns me lock, stock, and barrel. When sinners bow to His lordship, not only do they get saved, but their whole life comes under the Lord's direction. The Bible says we are bought with a price. He owns us, as we are told in 1 Corinthians 6:19, 20.

Long an opponent of lordship teaching, Charles Ryrie has made some strong and shocking statements in his book *Balancing the Christian Life* (Chicago: Moody, 1969). We have already noted his emphatic assertion that "the message of faith only and the message of faith plus commitment of life cannot both be the gospel" and that "therefore, one of them is false and comes under the curse of perverting the gospel or preaching another gospel" (p. 170).

Another dispensationalist, Ray Stanford, while president of a large dispensational Bible college, wrote a book with two of his colleagues (Seymore and Streib) entitled *Handbook of Personal Evangelism.* Here are some excerpts from their book ([Hollywood, Fla.: Florida Bible College, 1975], 91-95).

- "Lordship salvation contradicts scripture."
- "This message [lordship salvation] cannot save."
- "This message is accursed of God."
- "The person who preaches such a message is also accursed of God."
- "It hinders the growth of the body of Christ—this will stop the growth of the local churches."

It is because of the havoc dispensationalism has caused in American Christianity that I have an increasing conviction of the importance of this issue. Some who read this book may think we face a merely semantic problem, a simple failure in communicating with each other. Others may charge me of nit-picking or making too much of a fuss over small differences.

Listen carefully to my response. The issue before us is not minor. It goes to the very heart of the gospel. It truly is a question of who is preaching "another gospel." It is, as *Christianity Today* has described it, a "volcanic issue" (Sept. 22, 1989, p. 21). The lordship of Christ is the very root of biblical Christianity. Without it, dispensational antinomianism is spiritually bankrupt. But when we ask, Just what effect does the true, biblical lordship position have on real Christians? here are some answers:

1. It provides and provokes that which keeps us coming to Christ for fresh forgiveness and fresh assurance.

2. It kills spiritual pride—there can be no more super-class of spiritual (versus carnal) Christians.

3. It exalts Christ, acknowledging His throne rights.

4. It proves helpful and hopeful, to saint and sinner alike, to know a Christ who is Lord of *all* and to know that as Lord He has power to save and power to sanctify.

5. It has a profound effect upon our evangelism. No more wicked huckstering off some poor, impotent, pathetic Jesus. No more getting votes for Jesus. The gospel of Christ's lordship boxes sinners up to the power of Christ and the mercy of the One who is able and willing to save *all* who come to God by Him.

TWO

Lordship, Experience, and Interpretation

There is a danger of forming any doctrine from our experience. Consider the following example, which describes the experience of many:

> When I was young I accepted Christ as my personal Savior, and that experience had some influence on my life for a time, but I didn't really live an active Christian life for years. Later I was taught that Christ must be my Lord, and that the problem with my defeated life was that I had not submitted to Christ as my Lord when I trusted Him as my Savior. So I did just that— submitted to Christ as my Lord. And since that experience I have been living the Christian life on a different plane.

A "Second Conversion"?

We have all heard this kind of a testimony in many forms. However it is described and by whatever name it is called, it affirms a second conversion or a step of consecration. Some may describe it as being filled with the Spirit. Or they may call it the "deeper life," the "higher life," or the "victorious life." The Bible knows nothing of these terms. They describe a deep, wide, and distinct line between those who have suddenly attained a higher level of consecration and other Christians.

There is nothing new about this teaching. It is well known. Roman Catholic writers have often maintained that the church is divided into three classes: sinners, penitents, and saints. Nonlordship teachers likewise tell us there are three classes of people: the unconverted, the converted, and the partakers of the "higher life" of complete consecration. They also make distinctions between "natural man," "carnal Christians," and "spiritual Christians" (which I will discuss later). But whether this teaching is old or new—Roman Catholic or Protestant—it is utterly impossible to find in the Scriptures.

The Word of God always speaks of two, and only two, great divisions of mankind. It distinguishes between those who are spiritually alive and those who are dead in sin, the believer and the unbeliever, the converted and the unconverted, the travelers on the narrow way and the travelers on the broad way, the wise and the foolish, the children of God and the children of the Devil. *Within* each of these two great classes there are, doubtless, various measures of sin and of grace. But they are like the difference between the higher and lower ends of an inclined plane. *Between* these two great classes there is an enormous gulf. They are as distinct as life and death, light and darkness, heaven and hell.

Spiritual Classes, or Degrees of Growth?

Of a division into three classes of people the Word of God says nothing at all! And if the Bible does not speak of such divisions or a second conversion, I question the wisdom of our doing so.

The difference between one degree of grace and another may be vast, I fully concede. Spiritual life admits of growth, and believers should be continually urged on every account to grow in grace. But the theory of a sudden, mysterious transition of a believer into a state of blessedness and entire consecration I cannot accept. Gradual growth in grace, knowledge, faith, love, holiness, humility, spiritual-mindedness—all this I see clearly taught and urged in Scripture, as well as exemplified in the lives of many of God's saints. But instantaneous leaps from unconsecrated belief to total consecration I fail to see in the Bible.

What warrant is there for saying that a man can possibly be converted without being consecrated to God? Doubtless he will need to become *more* consecrated as grace increases. No Christian is fully yielded in this life; otherwise he or she would be sinless. Christians can point to times of fresh commitment, to fresh surrender, to stronger and more joyous assurance. They might also point to some backsliding in heart, periods of coldness and indifference. Some may lose assurance (though not their salvation). Many of us can relate times of crisis resulting in our falling backward or moving forward. Submitting to Christ's lordship is not a once-and-done experience; it is a lifelong process. But it is a process that begins at conversion. There is never a time in the true Christian's life when Christ is not his Lord.

The postponement of Jesus' lordship by means of a two-step salvation, a second conversion, has done great damage and caused many divisions in the Christian church. It has produced a generation of antinomian, self-deceived church members and has grossly diluted the meaning of true conversion. If a person is not consecrated to God on the very day he is born again and converted, what indeed does conversion mean?

Are not men in danger of undervaluing the immense blessedness of conversion? Are they not, when they urge believers on to the "higher life" of a second conversion, underrating the length and breadth and depth and height of that great first work of grace which Scripture depicts as the new birth, the new creation, the spiritual resurrection?

I have at times suspected that some people who speak glowingly of their "consecration" must have a singularly low, inadequate view of conversion, if indeed they understand conversion at all. It almost seems that when they were "consecrated," they were in reality *converted* for the first time! Someone who is genuinely converted does not need a second conversion. Nor should he expect that some day, by one enormous step, he will pass into a state of entire consecration in this life. I see no warrant for such teaching in Scripture. The tendency of such a doctrine is thoroughly mischievous, depressing the humble-minded and meek, and puffing up the shallow, the ignorant, and the self-conceited.

Experiences Misunderstood

There are several possible interpretations of second-step crisis experiences. On the one hand, a person may not have been truly saved in the first place. On the other hand, it is possible that the person lacked biblical assurance when he "accepted Christ as his personal Savior" (language that is foreign to the New Testament and subject to many different meanings). In either case, the person has misunderstood his experience.

That is why I emphasize that *we must interpret our experience by the Bible and not interpret the Bible by our experience.* Likewise, we must never invent doctrines on the basis of our experience.

One of the great dangers of personal testimonies is the interpretations that people attach to their experiences. I have heard many testimonies that, however sincere, offered interpretations of experience that were woefully unbiblical. Most of the second-work-of-grace testimonies involve erroneous interpretations of experience. Because many people do not interpret their first experience biblically, they consequently misinterpret their so-called second experience as well.

The Christian life involves many deep spiritual experiences subsequent to conversion. That is only normal. The wise believer is careful not to invent new doctrines or names to characterize these events. Particularly dangerous is the idea of a second conversion. It implies a two-level Christianity—a distinction between the haves and the have-nots among believers. The truth is that there are as many levels of Christianity as there are Christians at different stages of sanctification.

A word of caution is applicable to both nonlordship and lordship teachers. Both should be very slow to draw conclusions regarding the genuineness of other people's reported experiences. While nonlordship spokesmen may believe that both a first and a second "conversion" are genuine, lordship advocates may wrongly assume that neither experience is true. In reality, it may be a person's interpretation of his experiences that is suspect, not one or the other experience itself. With the Bible in hand, we should seek to correct erroneous interpretations of what may well be a true experience. We will only do that if we are careful, in both speaking and writing, to distinguish between the experience and the interpretation of the experience. In some cases both may be false, but in many cases an unbiblical interpretation is given to what is a genuine spiritual experience.

We must be cautious to remember that many true believers have a better experience with God than they have an understanding of how to formulate it. Let me illustrate.

I was preaching at a retreat on the topic of "Christ Our Prophet, Christ Our Priest, and Christ Our King." A young lady about eighteen years old came to speak to me at the end of the service. She told me that her father was a missionary and that he had never told her that she must trust Christ as Prophet, Priest, and King. She had come to Christ for forgiveness and salvation some years before but did not consciously trust Him as Prophet or King. I asked her about her experience. "Did you desire to be taught the will of Christ?" She answered, "Yes." "Did you desire for Him to reign over you and protect you from your enemies and His?" Again, she answered that she had. After talking with her a few minutes,

I had reason to believe that she was a devout Christian. So I said, "I'm confident from what you tell me that you have every reason to believe that your experience with Christ is genuine and that tonight your understanding caught up with your experience."

We all know Christians who give every evidence of being born again, though they could not define the theological term *regeneration*. Their experience is better than their understanding. John says in 1 John 5:12, "He who has the Son has life," and when we have Him, we have Him in all of His offices, all of His person, and all of His saving work—though we may not fully understand it.

It is important to make a distinction between: (1) a person who claims to be saved and lives like a saved person, yet does not fully understand the implications of Christ's lordship, and (2) the person who claims to be saved and satisfied but rejects the will of Christ, has no desire or intention to follow Jesus, and renounces any submission to Christ, His claims, or His authority as Teacher and King. The one case is a matter of misunderstanding. The other is antinomianism.

There should be no doubt that the first person has bowed to the lordship of Christ, though his understanding is very limited. But the second person has no reason to believe he is a Christian at all. Notice, I said, "no *reason* to believe" (assurance). That is as far as we can go in judging the matter. We cannot look into the Lamb's Book of Life. We cannot have Christ in halves or in parts.

"Personal Savior" but Not Lord?

It is sad that the language "trust Christ as your personal Savior," has crept into the Christian church in the last one hundred years and is common in present-day evangelism. It did not come from the New Testament, from the apostles, from the respected church fathers, or from the Reformers. It is not found in the Westminster Standards or the old Baptist confessions. You will not find it among the great preachers of the past—men such as Bunyan, Spurgeon, Whitefield, or Jonathan Edwards.

Such terminology and what it conveys has contributed to the lordship controversy. I personally do not like it, nor do I use it. Granted, if we have Christ, He is our personal Savior, our personal Prophet, our personal Priest, our personal King. But He is all of that together, or none of it at all.

Often those who testify of a second conversion refer to their first experience as "before I made Christ Lord." There is not a line in the Bible that supports such language or such a doctrine.

Imagine a supposed convert of the nonlordship teaching saying, "I am saved but Jesus is not my Lord" or, "I am saved but I have not submitted to Christ's lordship or His will for my life" or, "I am saved but I have no desire to be taught of Christ." The very thought is preposterous and totally foreign to biblical salvation.

That is far different from a new convert's not realizing all the implications of the lordship of Christ in every area of his life. The clear teaching of the Bible is that growing in grace is a lifetime process. And the desire to grow, the desire to obey, is inseparable from saving faith.

A Gospel of Obedience

The gospel of belief is also a gospel of obedience. John clearly says that obedience is one of the tests that believers might *know* they have eternal life. Hear his words in 1 John 2:3–5: "Now by this we know that we know Him, if we keep His commandments. He who says, 'I know Him,' and does not keep His commandments, is a liar, and the truth is not in him. But whoever keeps His word, truly the love of God is perfected in him. By this we know that we are in Him."

Paul also knew of the relationship between true believing and evangelical obedience when he said:

. . . and to give you who are troubled rest with us when the Lord Jesus is revealed from heaven with His mighty angels, in flaming fire taking vengeance on those who do not know God, and on those who *do not obey the gospel* of our Lord Jesus Christ. These shall be punished with everlasting destruction from the presence of the Lord and from the glory of His power. (2 Thess. 1:7–9, emphasis added)

We see it taught in Hebrews 5:8, 9: "Though He was a Son, yet He learned obedience by the things which He suffered. And having been perfected, He became the author of eternal salvation to all who obey Him." Yes, it is also a gospel of obedience. Jesus Himself put it succinctly: "If you love Me, keep My commandments" (John 14:15).

The hymn writer James H. Sammis had it straight when he wrote, "Trust and obey, for there's no other way to be happy in Jesus, but to trust and obey."

This is not works-salvation but works as a result of true believing, as a result of regeneration: "If anyone is in Christ, he is a new creation; old things have passed away; behold, all things have become new" (2 Cor. 5:17). The passage does not say that only some are new creatures, or that it would be nice if any in Christ were new creatures. Neither does it say that this new creation is optional or reserved only for those who later make Christ Lord of their lives. To be in Christ is to be a new creature. It is to have Christ as Savior and Lord.

THREE

Lordship, Nonlordship, and Dispensationalism

In chapter 1 I pointed out that the lordship controversy will never be settled unless we come to grips with the theology behind nonlordship teaching. The nonlordship position is just the tip of a theological iceberg, a product of a faulty philosophical system and the literal hermeneutic of dispensationalism.

I have noted that nonlordship is a child whose father is Arminianism and whose mother is dispensationalism. Nonlordship also has an aunt, antinomianism (who, like dispensationalism, opposes the law). There are also many cousins, some of which I will address in subsequent chapters.

As is the nonlordship teaching, so too the larger dispensational system of theology is diametrically opposed to that theology found in the pages of the Westminster Confession, the old Baptist Confession of 1689, and the Heidelberg Catechism. Dispensationalism would have been declared erroneous by the Synod of Dort, as was her husband Arminianism. Dispensational theology is nothing less than a frontal attack on covenantal and Reformed theology.

An Autobiographical Sketch

In this chapter I will address some of the doctrinal issues of dispensationalism. Perhaps a short autobiographical word may be helpful, to explain my own departure from dispensationalism. I especially want to express gratitude for the things I have learned, which have helped me on my way to the Celestial City, and to show respect to many who taught me to revere the Holy Scriptures. I want to be on record as acknowledging that the formative years of my spiritual development were under the ministry of godly men who were committed to dispensationalism. It was under such a ministry that I was taught the importance of a personal devotional life. I was taught to be missionary minded. I was taught to be a personal witness for Christ. I was taught five fundamentals of the faith: (1) the inspiration and infallibility of the Scriptures, (2) the virgin birth of Christ, (3) the miracles of Christ, (4) the substitutionary atonement of Christ, (5) the bodily resurrection of Christ.

One of the first books that had a profound effect on my methods of evangelism was *True Evangelism*, by Lewis Sperry Chafer. I can still recommend it as very helpful.

I did not find my way out of dispensationalism easily. Leaving took time and tears, and it cost me fellowship with some genuinely committed Christian friends. Some of them thought I was departing from the faith or going liberal. My inward heart-struggle to embrace the historic Christian faith involved not only intellectual conflict but also emotional struggles. The many changes were not made in haste, anger, passion, or ecstasy. It did not happen in a weekend. I had spent the first ten years of my Christian life immersed in dispensationalism. I had worn out three Scofield Bibles, and the fourth was falling apart. I had heard Lewis Sperry Chafer in person. The only systematic theology I had studied was Dr. Chafer's eight-volume set.

My theological change was the result of a serious, exhaustive search to know three things: What do the Scriptures say? What do they mean? How do I apply them to my belief and practice?

With this little history of my own journey in mind, I now pursue the rather difficult task of critiquing the principles of dispensationalism. My prayer is that I would do that without being disrespectful or uncharitable to the many genuine Christians who sincerely hold to this view, which I now consider erroneous, unbiblical, and dangerous.

Although I strongly differ with my dispensational brethren in their interpretation of Scripture, I would defend their right to be wrong. I do not wish to separate from their fellowship. No Christian wishes to be argumentative.

But it is impossible to address this controversial issue without being polemic and somewhat censorious of the system. I must be very candid and say that I cannot approach dispensationalism in an unbiased or dispassionate manner. I strongly believe it to be a departure from the historic faith of our fathers. We are now reaping some of the fruit of this unbiblical and unhistoric theology, especially in the work of evangelism (justification) and in teaching on the Christian life (sanctification).

Defining Dispensationalism

It is impossible to give one succinct definition of dispensationalism today because of the many changes that have occurred among dispensational teachers. The old definition of "dispensation" found in the Scofield Bible will no longer suffice: "A dispensation is a period of time during which a man is tested in respect of obedience to some specific revelation of the will of God" (Scofield Reference Bible, 5, note 4).

Recently I read a review of John H. Gerstner's book *Wrongly Dividing the Word of Truth,* in which Gerstner exposes the errors and dangers of dispensationalism. The reviewer, Tom Wells, made an excellent observation that will underscore my premise that it is impossible to give a concise definition of dispensationalism. Referring to dispensationalism, the reviewer said that though the author had done his home-work, he was shooting at a moving target. It is no longer possible to speak of dispensationalism as a unit. In the earlier days the system had various varieties and offshoots, but if Darby, Scofield, or even Chafer were to return today, they would be bewildered by the various stances of those still called "dispensationalists." The reviewer was correct when he referred to dispensationalism as a moving target. It certainly has been on the move. The question is, What will the next move be?

Dispensationalism, Arminianism, and antinomianism wear many masks, and there are many degrees and shades, as well as extremes, among all three. Although the dispensational position is complex and hard to pin down, and their scholars have modified their views over time, I think I am safe in giving the following description for our purpose in this study.

Dispensationalists divide history into a number of distinct epochs during each of which God works out a particular phase of His overall plan. Each particular phase or dispensation represents a distinctive way in which God exercises His government over the world and tests human obedience. Beyond this, dispensationalists differ on a number of issues, for example, the relationship between Israel and the church: Hyper-dispensationalism is characterized by such distinctives as the view that the church did not begin until the middle of the Book of Acts. The classical dispensationalism of C. I. Scofield, Lewis Sperry Chafer, and others of the old school held that Israel is on earth, the church is in heaven, and never the twain shall meet. The neo-dispensationalist view is promoted by such leaders as Charles C. Ryrie, Dwight Pentecost, and Zane C. Hodges. They hold that the church and Israel shall come together after the millennium. Each of these views has many other distinctives, but this is not meant to be an in-depth study. The differences shown here simply illustrate that there are varieties of dispensationalism.

Distinguishing Features of Dispensationalism

Charles C. Bass, in his excellent book *Backgrounds to Dispensationalism* (Grand Rapids: Eerdmans, 1960), identifies some of the distinguishing features of dispensationalism (pp. 13–46):

- The nature and purpose of a dispensation
- The literal interpretation of Scripture
- The dichotomy between Israel and the church
- A restricted view of the church
- A Jewish concept of the kingdom
- A postponed kingdom
- The distinction between law and grace
- The compartmentalization of Scripture
- The pretribulation rapture
- The purpose of the Great Tribulation
- The nature of the millennial reign of Christ
- The eternal state
- The apostate nature of Christendom

Dispensationalism and covenant theology differ on many biblical doctrines, such as:

- The grace of God
- The law of God
- The church of God
- The Word of God (interpretation)
- Living the Christian life
- World-and-life view
- Sanctification (whether by a fixed, objective standard of righteousness)
- Eschatology

Although there are many important differences, four major differences go to the heart of dispensationalism. We could call them the four main pillars.

Four Pillars of Dispensationalism

1. The first pillar of dispensationalism is its *literalism and Jewish understanding of the Old Testament prophecy and the messianic kingdom*.

2. The second is the *parenthesis theory of the kingdom and the church*. According to this theory, the church age is an unforeseen parenthesis in the Jewish program as described by Old Testament prophets. If the Jews had not rejected Jesus, the Jewish kingdom would have begun at our Lord's first coming. But, God's "Plan A" failed, or was thwarted, or interrupted, and the church age—totally unforeseen by the Old Testament prophets—was interjected as "Plan B," a substitute for "Plan A." The dispensationalists call this the "parenthetical church age."

My Bible knows nothing about a God who does not have power to perform His plan. The God of the Bible is sovereign in creation, sovereign in redemption, and sovereign in providence. He is all-wise in planning and all powerful in performing. We must ask the dispensational teachers the following questions about their parenthesis theory: If the church is a parenthesis, when did it begin, and how do you know? When will it end, and how do you know?

3. The third pillar of the dispensational system, which most dispensationalists apparently have not seriously examined, is the *dichotomy between Old Testament Israel and the New Testament church*. Dispensationalism teaches that the Old Testament saints are not now in the church universal, which is the body of Christ.

4. The fourth pillar of this erroneous teaching, which bears most heavily on the lordship controversy, is its *false antithesis between the law and the gospel*. The moral law (the Ten Commandments) according to dispensational teaching today is but the quenching fire and cooling ashes of a former religion.

Biblically, however, the moral law carries permanent validity and goes straight to the root of our modern problems, laying its finger on the church's deepest need in evangelism and in the Christian life, that is, sanctification. The moral law also addresses our deepest needs in society, for we live in a lawless age. We have lawlessness in the home, in the schools, in government, and in the church. We are in need of a common set of rules for action—the duties and prohibitions contained in both the gospel and the law.

The law by which God rules us is as dear to Him as the gospel by which He saves us. God's law should be dear to us as well. Charles Haddon Spurgeon, that great preacher and soul winner, in a sermon called *The Perpetuity of the Law of God* (*The Metropolitan Tabernacle*, vol. 28, sermon 1660 [Edinburgh: Banner of Truth, 1971]), said:

> Very great mistakes have been made about the law. Not long ago there were those about us who affirmed that the law is utterly abrogated and abolished, and they openly taught that believers were not bound to make the moral law a rule for their lives. What would have been sin in other men, they counted as no sin in themselves. From such Antinomianism as that, may God deliver us. We are not under the law as the method of salvation, but we delight to see the law in the hand of Christ, and desire to obey the Lord in all things.

The dispensationalists would not agree with Charles Bridges concerning the relationship between the law and the gospel. In his classic book *The Christian Ministry* ([London: Banner of Truth, 1958], 222), Bridges wrote:

> The mark of a minister "approved unto God, a workman that needeth not to be ashamed," is, that he, "rightly divides the word of truth." This implies a full and direct application of the gospel to the mass of his unconverted hearers, combined with a body of spiritual instruction to the several classes of Christians.

His system will be marked by scriptural symmetry and comprehensiveness. It will embrace the whole revelation of God, in its doctrinal instruction, experimental privileges, and practical results. This revelation is divided into two parts—the law and the gospel—essentially distinct from each other, though so intimately connected, that an accurate knowledge of neither can be obtained without the other.

Dispensationalists set up a false antithesis between law and grace. (Of course when we are talking about how a person is justified, there is real antithesis, and every Christian should recognize this. Justification is by grace alone, not by works of the law.) The dispensational error in regard to the law is twofold. First, it applies this sharp antithesis to the successive dispensations, interpreting the Mosaic Law as *law in contrast with grace,* and the gospel dispensation as *grace in contrast with law.* Second, this antithesis leads dispensationalism into a false view of the law within the sphere of grace. This erroneous view appears very clearly in the Scofield Reference Bible (pp. 999–1000, 1002) and in Chafer's *Systematic Theology* (8 vols. [Dallas, 1948], 4:180–251).

Many true Christians traveling on the road to the Celestial City grow very weary and discouraged with the divisions and controversies they encounter along the way. Christian, you must remember that God brings good out of evil. The Cross is the best illustration of this principle. The most wicked thing that was ever done by the hands of men was crucifying our Lord; yet the greatest blessings that God ever gave us are the blessings that flow from the Cross.

We can take encouragement from these words of an old Puritan:

The road to heaven is very narrow, and worse yet, there is a dangerous ditch on either side of that narrow road. On the one side is the ditch of DESPAIR and on the other side there is the ditch of PRE-

SUMPTION, but bless God, in front of the ditch of Despair is a hedgerow of God's promises and in front of the ditch of Presumption is a hedgerow of God's precepts.

FOUR

The Beginnings of Dispensationalism in America

In chapter 3 we considered the vital relationship of dispensationalism to the lordship controversy. Dispensationalism is the theological mother of nonlordship teaching. In this study I wish to give a very brief history of dispensationalism in the United States.

I am taking this little diversion because many if not most people who carry Scofield Bibles and sit under dispensational teachers know very little about the system and its history. They are unaware of how the dispensational theological system differs from historic Reformational theology in general and Reformed, covenantal theology in particular. Not only people in the pews but often the preachers themselves have never seriously compared dispensationalism with covenant theology as it is most clearly expressed in the Westminster Confession of Faith and the Heidelberg Catechism. Covenant theology is the arch rival of dispensationalism.

It is my conviction that many who are presently disposed toward dispensationalism would not be if they were better informed about that system and its history—its theological roots and the doctrinal errors it has spawned.

The Roots of Dispensationalism

Dispensationalism has its roots in the Plymouth Brethren Movement, which began in the United Kingdom. Writers differ as to time and place where the Brethren Movement began. The first "breaking of bread service" I can find a record of was in 1827 in Dublin. The best information points to John Nelson Darby as a key founder and early teacher of the Brethren Movement. There are other names associated very early, such as A. N. Groves, B. W. Newton, W. H. Dorman, E. Cronin, and J. G. Bullett. These men were early leaders in places like Dublin, Plymouth, and Bristol. It is generally agreed that Darby was the energizing and guiding spirit in the movement's beginning, despite many differences and divisions among these men in the early days and thereafter.

Some dispensationalists deny a connection with this movement. But their arguments will not survive historical examination. Dispensationalism is indeed a development of the Plymouth Brethren Movement, growing into a theological system and a method of biblical interpretation during the late nineteenth century.

The first record of dispensationalism in the United States is when J. N. Darby twice visited the U.S. in 1864–65. Through two visits to the 16th and Walnut Avenue Presbyterian Church in St. Louis, then pastored by Dr. James H. Brooks, this church became the principal center of dispensationalism in America. For a Presbyterian church to promote dispensationalism was like mixing oil with water. But Dr. Brooks quickly became Darby's most prominent supporter and is said to be the father of dispensationalism in the United States.

Brooks propagated dispensationalism by his own Bible studies with young men. His best-known student was C. I. Scofield. Brooks published many books and pamphlets (this should teach us the power of literature) and edited a magazine called *The Truth*. A line of influence can be traced from Darby to Brooks, from Brooks to Scofield, from Scofield to Chafer, and from Chafer to Dallas.

Inroads into Mainline Churches

To understand Dr. Brooks's conversion to dispensationalism, it may be wise to call attention to conditions in the mainline denominations in the U.S. at the time. In the early 1900s liberalism was beginning to rear its ugly head in mainline churches. This sad condition had a profound effect on the success and inroads of dispensationalism. Initially, liberal Presbyterians were more influenced by dispensationalism than other denominations. Princeton Theological Seminary, once the stronghold of biblical Christianity worldwide, was one of the first places where liberalism surfaced. In 1914 J. Ross Stevenson became president of Princeton Seminary. Dr. Stevenson was more interested in ecumenical goals than the theology of the Westminster Standards. Eventually a group of spiritual and theological giants followed J. Gresham Machen to found a new seminary. On September 25, 1929, Westminster Theological Seminary, with fifty students and a choice faculty, was opened. There has never been a faculty like it since.

Westminster's faculty consisted of articulate Reformed theologians. They were fighting for the fundamentals of the faith, namely, the inspiration of the Scriptures, the virgin birth of Christ, the bodily resurrection of Christ, the miracles of Christ, and the substitutionary atonement. Their battle was against liberalism, and similar battles were being fought in most, if not all, the mainline denominations. Those who rejected liberalism and held to the five fundamentals mentioned above were labeled "fundamentalists."

Their fundamentalism should not be confused with the present-day dispensational fundamentalism. Let me explain. The five fundamentals mentioned above are beliefs of historic Christianity. In that sense every true Christian who embraces those truths is a fundamentalist. Present-day dispensational fundamentalists, though holding to those five essential truths, often attack many other important fundamentals of the faith that Reformed people have always cherished and have shed their blood to defend.

Scofield dispensationalism brought a new kind of fundamentalism into many churches, which filled a vacuum created by liberalism. The churches had drifted away from the doctrinal roots expressed in the old confessions and creeds. Many of the best schools and seminaries had been taken over by liberals and modernists. Their influence was felt first in the colleges, then in the seminaries, then in the pulpits, and finally in the pews. Bible-believing Christians had to turn to new teachers who held the Bible in high esteem. The vacuum left by liberalism provided a prime opportunity for the entrance and spread of the new dispensational teaching.

This development produced the independent church movement, the independent Bible conference movement, and the Bible school movement. Their members were almost all carrying Scofield Bibles, and their leaders were predominantly dispensational in their views.

The major training center for evangelical and Bible-believing churches was Dallas Theological Seminary, founded in 1924, with Lewis Sperry Chafer as its first president. In that desperate hour, when the crucial battle between modernism and historic Christianity was being waged, sincere, Bible-believing people turned to Dallas, the mecca of dispensationalism, for teaching on God's Word. Subsequently, many dispensational Bible schools and colleges were born during this period—all unreformed.

The late Robert K. Churchill, a respected Presbyterian minister, wrote a little paperback, *Lest We Forget* (Philadelphia: Orthodox Presbyterian Church, 1986), reflecting on the first fifty years of the Orthodox Presbyterian Church. Churchill confirms what I have said about dispensational inroads into the Presbyterian Church (U.S.A.) (pp. 29–40). He tells of his personal experience in two Presbyterian churches: the First Presbyterian Church of Tacoma, Washington, where he was converted, baptized, and called to the ministry, and a congregation in neighboring Seattle. Churchill explains how in these two great churches the notes in the Scofield Reference Bible became more and more prominent in the preaching. He laments, "These notes, and the interpretation of Scripture upon which they were based, were contrary to our presbyterian and Reformed heritage" (p. 28).

Churchill (p. 32) tells of Dr. Chafer's delivering a series of lectures on the subject of grace (the same material now in Chafer's book entitled *Grace*).

> But Chafer's treatment of the subject of grace never arrives at the right view of the law of God. According to Dr. Chafer, the law was a condition of salvation placed upon the people of God in the Old Testament during a special and limited time period—the Dispensation of Law. This condition, Chafer contended, no longer has application to the New Testament believer since we relate to God under a new dispensation, the Dispensation of Grace. Since, as he put it, "we are no longer under law, but under grace," Chafer argued that there is no necessary relationship between law and grace. Here is law without grace, and grace without law. Always and in every sense, law and grace are opposed to each other.
>
> This teaching appears to be scriptural, but in reality it was the ancient error of antinomianism (antilaw) which denies that the law has application to the Christian. Chafer defended this view by means of a radical reinterpretation of the Scriptures.

Not a Return to Historic Truth

How could dispensationalism be welcomed and embraced in strong Presbyterian churches whose Confession of Faith teaches Reformed, Calvinistic, covenant theology? Though there is no simple answer, one thing is certain. The churches were no longer teaching these doctrinal distinctives of their own Confession.

All honest dispensationalists would agree that the dispensational system of theology has a different view of the grace of God, the law of God, the church of God, the inter-pretation of the Word of God, and the salvation of God—different from the tested, respected, historic creeds and con-fessions. Likewise, dispensationalism has a different view of living the Christian life, that is, of sanctification, and of how justification and sanctification are inseparably joined to-gether in the application of God's salvation.

We cannot overlook the accomplishments of dispensa-tionalism. It has given rise to Bible colleges and independent churches all over the land. It has spawned numerous inde-pendent missions, independent preachers, and missionaries. If we apply the pragmatic test and ask, "Does it work?" the answer is yes; it has seen much growth and success. If we apply the same test and ask the same question of

- the Watchtower, the answer would be yes, it works;
- Mormonism, the answer would be yes, it works;
- Roman Catholicism, the answer would be yes, it works;
- the charismatic movement, the answer would be yes, it works.

They all have numerous converts and followers. They build schools and churches, and have missionaries and great accomplishments. But, there is another, more important ques-tion that needs to be asked. Are they true? Is what they teach biblical? This question will bring a different answer.

Dispensationalism represents no minor difference from historic Reformed teachings. It is not just a difference in end-times theories. It is a whole system of theology that touches every major doctrine of Christianity. What is at stake is the saving gospel of Jesus Christ and the sinner's assurance that he is living according to God's plan for history.

FIVE

The Nature of
Saving Faith

Nearly five hundred years ago, late in October of 1517, a young Augustinian monk, professor of theology, and pastor in Wittenberg, Germany, in the fire of his zeal for Christian truth, nailed 95 theses to the door of the Castle Church. His name was Martin Luther. He had left the study of law and entered the priesthood seeking to be justified before God. As a result of studying the Scriptures, he discovered the biblical truths that had long been covered and obscured by the ritual and rubble of Rome. One of the great truths then restored to the church was justification by faith alone.

The Reality of False Faith

The issue before us in this chapter is not the denial of justification by faith alone but the perversion of that doctrine. Nonlordship teaching often excludes the possibility of spurious faith. And yet, religious deception is the worst kind of deception because of its eternal consequences. We must distinguish properly between justifying faith and spurious or counterfeit faith.

The Bible very clearly warns against spurious faith. Therefore, I wish to direct attention to its warnings and note some differences between spurious and true believers. I intend to cite biblical cases of spurious faith, thereby showing that the Scriptures teach the existence of belief that is not saving faith. I will also define true faith and give biblical examples of that faith which savingly joins one to Jesus Christ for all eternity.

With your Bible in hand, consider carefully the following contrasts.

There is a hope that shall perish: "The hope of the hypocrite shall perish" (Job 8:13); and there is a hope that "maketh not ashamed" (Rom. 5:5, KJV). Likewise, there is a faith that saves and a faith that damns. The need to distinguish between the two is vital in the contemporary church and central to the lordship controversy.

"There is a generation that is pure in its own eyes, yet is not washed from its filthiness" (Prov. 30:12). "There is a way which seems right to a man, but its end is the way of death" (Prov. 14:12). "You search the Scriptures, for in them you think you have eternal life; and these are they which testify of Me. But you are not willing to come to Me . . ." (John 5:39, 40).

These sobering passages have a pointed application to church membership today. I confess that I write this with feelings of sorrow and grief because the church is filled with many, many who give no biblical evidence of real conversion. There is an Athenian love of religious novelty and excitement, and a morbid distaste for anything old and regular— the well-beaten paths of our forefathers (cf. Jer. 6:16). There is much false faith today.

What is the difference between spurious faith and justifying faith, between false believers and true believers? Many differences could be considered, but the following four serve to separate the wheat from the chaff, the genuine from the counterfeit.

Four Differences Between False and True Faith

1. The first difference is that *spurious believers want Christ, but not without exception.* They want the grace of Christ, but not

the government of Christ—like the prodigal son who wanted his father's goods but not his father's rule. They desire the benefits of the Cross without bowing to the implications of the Crown. They want to go to heaven but not by the narrow way that leads there. They desire the free gift of eternal life but will not receive it with empty hands. Yes, they want Christ, but not without exception. They want Christ and their other lovers also. They want to be saved from the consequences of sin, but not from sin itself.

But our Lord came to save from sin. That is clear from the very first chapter of the New Testament. "You shall call His name Jesus: for He will save His people from their sins" (Matt. 1:21). Not *in* their sins but *from* their sins. Jesus is not just a hell insurance policy but the Savior from sin and its consequences—not just the consequences, but sin itself.

True saving faith wants Christ without exception. This is illustrated by our Lord's parables in Matthew 13.

> The kingdom of heaven is like treasure hidden in a field, which a man found and hid; and for joy over it he goes and sells all that he has and buys that field. Again, the kingdom of heaven is like a merchant seeking beautiful pearls, who, when he had found one pearl of great price, went and sold all that he had, and bought it. (Matt. 13:44–46)

The treasure and the pearl is Christ; and saving faith wants Him without exception.

2. The second difference between spurious believers and true believers is that *true believers want Christ as He is set forth in the Scriptures;* that is, as the only Mediator between God and man (1 Tim. 2:5). As Mediator, Christ has three offices: *Prophet, Priest, and King* of His church.

As Priest, Christ procures pardon and peace by His sacrifice on the Cross and maintains peace by His intercession for His sheep. "I pray for them. I do not pray for the world but for those whom You have given Me; for they are Yours.

And all Mine are Yours, and Yours are Mine; and I am glorified in them" (John 17:9, 10). As Prophet, Christ is wisdom, teacher, and counselor in all things. As anointed King, Christ rules and reigns over the true believer in all things and protects him from all his enemies.

Spurious believers want Christ only as a Priest to procure pardon and peace, but not as a Prophet to instruct them or as a King to rule over them. We are not saved, however, by one of the offices of Christ, but by Him. "He who has the Son has life" (1 John 5:12). If we have Him, we must have Him in all of His offices, as He is set forth in the Bible.

The Westminster divines and our Baptist fathers taught these truths to Christians and their children. However, you will never hear them from nonlordship teachers. They show little or no respect for what the Holy Spirit taught our forefathers concerning the lordship of Christ. They seem only concerned about His priestly office. If they were straight on the following questions and answers (from the Westminster Larger Catechism), they would never separate the offices of Christ, or His lordship from His saviorhood.

Q. 41. *Why was our Mediator called Jesus?*

A. Our Mediator was called Jesus, because he saveth his people from their sins.

Q. 42. *Why was our Mediator called Christ?*

A. Our Mediator was called Christ, because he was anointed with the Holy Ghost above measure; and so set apart, and fully furnished with all authority and ability, to execute the offices of prophet, priest, and king of his church, in the estate both of his humiliation and exaltation.

Q. 43. *How doth Christ execute the office of a prophet?*

A. Christ executeth the office of a prophet, in his revealing to the church, in all ages, by his Spirit and word, in divers ways of administration, the whole will of God, in all things concerning their edification and salvation. . . .

Q. 45. *How doth Christ execute the office of a king?*

A. Christ executeth the office of a king, in calling out of the world a people to himself, and giving them officers, laws, and censures, by which he visibly governs them; in bestowing saving grace upon his elect, rewarding their obedience, and correcting them for their sins, preserving and supporting them under all their temptations and sufferings, restraining and overcoming all their enemies, and powerfully ordering all things for his own glory, and their good; and also in taking vengeance on the rest, who know not God, and obey not the gospel.

3. The third difference is that *spurious believers never acknowledge the inconveniences that follow a commitment to Christ* (and believe me, there are some!). They want Christ, but they have never done what Jesus commanded, that is, *counted the cost* (Luke 14:25–33). Every serious Christian knows that the Christian life is not a gospel hay ride. All is not "happy, happy, happy" all the time. The language of the Christian life is also "I war," "I fight," "I wrestle," "I strive." Jesus was honest about this at the outset of His gospel invitation. Any serious study of Luke 9 and 14 will underscore just how honest Jesus was in inviting men to follow Him.

In Luke 9:57 a would-be follower said to Jesus, "Lord, I will follow You wherever You go." Most modern evangelists would have signed him up immediately and baptized him the same day; and he would have been teaching Sunday school in two weeks. But what did Jesus do? He was honest. He said to him, "Foxes have holes and birds of the air have nests, but the Son of Man has nowhere to lay His head" (v. 58). This may not have been a very good way to amass followers, but it was truthful. Jesus was honest at the outset. "If any man will come after me, let him deny himself, and take up his cross daily, and follow me" (Luke 9:23). This invitation is not for some second work of grace or second act of consecration. It is the initial invitation to salvation.

37

True faith wants Christ and all the inconveniences that necessarily follow. It costs to be a Christian. I am not talking about the price of redemption. That is infinite—we are redeemed by the precious blood of Christ, nothing less. I am talking about what it costs to live a Christian life. It costs you nothing to *become* a Christian; but it may cost you everything to be a Christian. The gospel motto is "without money and without price" (Isa. 55:1). We are "justified freely by His grace through the redemption that is in Christ Jesus" (Rom. 3:24). Yet, for all that, if a man will live the Christian life, it will cost him something.

Consider for a moment a blind man sitting by the wayside, begging. He asks to have his eyes opened. Will it cost him anything? No, the Savior would not accept all the gold in the world for the cure. He will freely open his eyes. But when they are opened, it will cost that blind man something. Once he has obtained his sight he will be called upon to discharge the duties of one who has eyes. He will no longer be allowed to sit there and beg. If he tries to do so, he will lose the sympathy that is bestowed upon the blind. Once his eyes are opened he must use them and earn his own bread. His receiving sight will cost him something, for he will now be conscious of the darkness of the night, of which he knew nothing before. And there are sad sights he now must look upon that never grieved him before, for often what the eye does not see, the heart does not mourn.

True religion is a costly thing, but it is also a lasting thing. It lasts for life. False religion comes and goes. True regeneration is never repeated; it is the beginning of a life that will know no end, either in time or eternity.

Peter wrote, "Therefore, brethren, be even more diligent to make your calling and election sure, for if you do these things you will never stumble" (2 Peter 1:10). Dr. John Brown, godly minister and theologian of Edinburgh, Scotland, commenting on this verse, said, "If we would prove to the world and to our own hearts that we are the called and elect of God, we must be and do what the called and elect of God are called

38

to be and to do" (*Commentary on 2 Peter* [Edinburgh, Scotland: William Olephant & Sons, n.d.], 65). We could say it another way; that is, that if I would prove to the world and to my own heart that I am a Christian, I must be and do what Christians are meant to be and do—and that will cost something.

4. The fourth difference between spurious and true believers is that *the spurious believer's heart is not changed and therefore his faith is not operative*. Simon Magus "believed" and "was baptized," but his heart was not right in the sight of God. He was in the gall of bitterness, and Peter told him he would perish with his money, despite his outward belief and baptism (Acts 8:13, 21). *True faith is operative, purifying the heart* (Acts 15:8, 9).

In summary:

1. Saving faith wants Christ without exception.
2. Saving faith receives Christ in all of His offices—as Prophet, Priest, and King.
3. Saving faith receives Christ and all the inconveniences that follow.
4. Saving faith is operative, purifying the heart.

None of these things is true of spurious faith.

We must properly distinguish between justifying faith and spurious faith. The nonlordship teaching fails miserably on this point. The consequences of remaining in deception are too enormous to neglect self-examination. Since there is a faith that will not save, men must be warned of its fatal consequences. We are justified by faith alone, but true faith has distinguishing traits. That faith which is alone is not the kind of faith that justifies. Because of the danger of being deceived the apostle Paul told the Corinthians to examine themselves as to whether they are in the faith (2 Cor. 13:5). All those on our church rolls would do well to do likewise.

John, in his first letter, gives some tests of eternal life, which we might call the "birthmarks" of the second birth. One of these birthmarks is belief or faith. "Whoever believes that Jesus is the Christ is born of God" (1 John 5:1). This saving belief is in the whole Christ, the Christ of the Bible—the only Mediator who right now is Prophet, Priest, and King of His church.

Saving faith reaches the whole man. It reaches his mind (what he thinks), his emotions or affections (what he feels), and his will (how he makes decisions and acts). Whatever else true religion is, it cannot be less than this:

- Right thinking in relationship to God.
- Right feeling in relationship to God.
- Right acting in relationship to God.

Nonlordship teachers seem to miss this salient point, settling for a change of mind not necessarily resulting in a change of conduct or direction. They say nothing about a changed will. Consider this explanation of repentance from Stanford, Seymore, and Streib, *Handbook of Personal Evangelism* (Hollywood, Fla.: Florida Bible College, 1975): "Any teaching that demands a change of conduct toward either God or man for salvation is to add works or human effort to faith, and this contradicts all scripture and is an accursed message."

No, saving faith is far more than intellectual assent to historical facts of the gospel. We can learn religious facts without the Spirit. We can memorize biblical facts just the same as we can learn math or English or history. But true faith is more.

First, this saving belief is revealed and applied by the Holy Spirit in regeneration (John 3:3). Second, this belief is expressed by the sinner in his response to the Savior. Third, this belief is made apparent in its fruit—repentance toward God and faith toward our Lord Jesus Christ (Acts 20:20, 21).

Several Varieties of Faith

Leading theologians of the past recognized that the Bible distinguishes between spurious faith and saving faith. The great

Princetonian, Charles Hodge, in his *Systematic Theology* (3:67–68), spoke of historical or speculative faith, temporary faith, and saving faith. Robert Dabney, a noted southern Presbyterian theologian, differentiated temporary faith, historical faith, miraculous faith, and saving faith. A former student of Hodge's at Princeton, James P. Boyce, who became one of the greatest Southern Baptist systematic theologians and principal founder of their first seminary, spoke of implicit faith, historical faith, temporary or delusive faith, and saving faith. The following distinctions summarize his discussions in his *Abstract of Systematic Theology* ([Reprint: Escondido, Calif.: den Dulk Christian Foundation], 389–94).

Historical faith. This faith is mere mental assent to the truths taught in the Scriptures as historical facts. It concurs that there was such a person as Jesus, who being the Son of God, wrought salvation and has commanded all men to repent and be baptized for the remission of sins. Such was the faith of Simon Magus (Acts 8:13–24). Judas also possessed a bare historical faith. But true saving faith is a work of the heart, as is manifest from the following passages: "Now when they heard this, they were cut to the heart" (Acts 2:37); "Believe in your heart that God has raised Him from the dead. . . . with the heart one believes to righteousness" (Rom. 10:9, 10).

Temporary or delusive faith. Such faith has many marks of true saving faith. It is not only an intellectual reception of the historical facts but a joyful acceptance of them. "The ones on the rock are those who, when they hear, receive the word with joy; and these have no root, who believe for a while and in time of temptation fall away" (Luke 8:13). Temporary faith soon falters. Its dubious nature becomes evident by its lacking the following characteristics of saving faith:

1. Continuance in trusting Christ, and in devotion to Him and His service.
2. Desire to be useful in the work of Christ.
3. Attendance to Christian duty.

4. Love of prayer, the Word of God, and worship with His people.
5. Devoted love of the children of God.
6. Progress in knowledge of self and sin and of Christ as Savior.
7. Progress in loving holiness and hating sin, with increased conviction of and humility concerning sinfulness.

Since Dr. Boyce is biblically correct in stating that temporary faith and delusive faith lack these seven things, the question that should concern every serious person is, Am I in possession of these characteristics of true saving faith?

Examples of Spurious Faith

Nonlordship teachers seem to ignore the fact that the Bible speaks of a spurious faith that does not save. Zane Hodges denies that the Bible says anything concerning two kinds of faith. He refuses to distinguish between what might be called a mere "mental faith" and a true faith. Yet the Scriptures give clear examples of false faith.

I have already mentioned the case of Simon Magus, of whom it is written, "Then Simon himself also *believed;* and when he was baptized he continued with Philip" (Acts 8:13). Simon expressed such apparent faith that Philip took him to be a genuine Christian and admitted him to Christian privileges. Yet Peter later told Simon that he would perish with his money, warning him: "You have neither part nor portion in this matter, for your heart is not right in the sight of God. . . . I see that you are poisoned by bitterness and bound by iniquity" (Acts 8:21, 23).

A man may believe *all* the truth contained in Scripture, so far as he is acquainted with it; indeed, he may be familiar with far more truth that many genuine Christians. And as his knowledge may be more extensive, so his faith may be more comprehensive. He may go even as far as Paul had. Although he believed all the Scripture before his conversion, his faith was not saving faith. Consider also Agrippa, to whom Paul said: "King Agrippa, do you believe the prophets? I know that you do *believe*" (Acts 26:27). But such faith did not save him.

James speaks of "dead faith" (James 1:17, 26), mere mental assent to certain historical facts. He also speaks of the belief of demons or devils (James 2:19). The demons have a sound confession, a religious appropriation of these facts. They believe in a person ("Jesus, You Son of God") and the power of Christ ("Have You come here to torment us?")(Matt. 8:29). But surely dead faith or devils' faith does not save.

The Seriousness of Spurious Faith

It is indeed sobering to discover how often the Bible speaks of unsaved people having faith in the Lord. Though it seems incredible, many are willing to have Christ as their Savior but are reluctant to submit to Him as their Lord, to be at His command, and to be governed by His laws. But more shocking still, there are unregenerate persons who profess Christ as Lord and yet are not in possession of saving faith. The scriptural proof of this assertion is found in Matthew 7:22–23: "Many will say to Me in that day, 'Lord, Lord, have we not prophesied in Your name, cast out demons in Your name, and done many wonders in Your name?' And then I will declare to them, I never knew you; depart from Me, you who practice lawlessness!" Here is a large class of people ("many") who profess Christ as Lord, do many mighty works in His name, and thus can even show their faith by their works— and yet theirs is not saving faith. They will hear Jesus say, "Depart from Me."

It is alarming to see how far nonsaving faith can go and how closely it can resemble true saving faith. Saving faith has Christ as its object; but so has spurious faith: "Many believed in His name when they saw the signs which He did. But Jesus did not commit Himself to them, because He knew all men" (John 2:23, 24). Saving faith is wrought by the Holy Spirit; but so also spurious faith has an apparent spirituality and may even partake to some degree of illuminating grace (Heb. 6:4). Then too, saving faith receives the Word of God; but so also does spurious faith: "He who received the seed on stony places, this is he who hears the word and immediately receives it with joy; yet he has no root in himself, but endures only for a while" (Matt. 13:20–21). Moreover, saving faith will cause people to prepare for the coming of the Lord; but so will spurious faith. Both the foolish and the wise virgins had the lamp of profession—they all trimmed their lamps and said "Lord, Lord"—but half of them heard the answer, "I do not know you" (Matt. 25:1–13). Furthermore, saving faith is accompanied by joy; but so is spurious faith: "The ones on the rock . . . receive the word with joy . . . who believe for a while and in the time of temptation fall away" (Luke 8:13).

When we realize how far spurious faith can go in its counterfeits, we are prone to say, "All this is very unsettling and confusing." Yes, it is distressing! But, if you value your soul or care for the souls of others, you will not dismiss this subject lightly. Since the Bible teaches that there is a faith in Christ that does not save and that it is easy to be deceived, you must earnestly seek the help of the Spirit. He Himself cautions us at this very point: "A deceived heart has turned him aside" (Isa. 44:20); "The pride of your heart has deceived you" (Obad. 3). "Take heed that you not be deceived" (Luke 21:8).

Failure to recognize the Bible's teaching on counterfeit faith has led to other errors. The tendency is to treat spurious believers as saved but not consecrated or not filled with the Spirit. This folly is often compounded by calling those who give no evidence of saving faith "carnal Christians," since they do not act like Christians (I will address this error later). The solution to this anomaly is often sought in some kind of second work of grace. Thus there is constant appeal to "carnal Christians" to fully surrender to Christ's lordship and be filled with the Spirit, when the problem is that, in most cases, they are spurious believers.

The Actions and Desires of Saving Faith

True justifying faith is, in the Lord's deep wisdom and condescension, variously expressed in Scripture according to its different actions, motions, and inclinations toward God. It is sometimes spoken of as a desire for union with God in Christ—as a *willing*: "And whosoever will, let him take the water of life freely" (Rev. 22:17, KJV). Scripture also speaks of *looking* to Him: "Look to Me, and be saved, all the ends of the earth" (Isa. 45:22). This text was used of God in Spurgeon's conversion. "Looking" may be the weakest act of faith.

True faith is also expressed as *hungering* and *thirsting* after righteousness (Matt. 5:6). To the soul that is hungry and thirsty for something that will everlastingly satisfy, Christ Jesus is milk, wine, water, the Bread of life, and the true manna (Isa. 55:1–2; John 6:48, 51). True faith will *"come, buy and eat"* and *drink* abundantly (Isa. 55:1; John 6:53–56). To the soul that is pursued by guilt and is not able to withstand the charge, Christ Jesus is the city of refuge. The poor guilty man exercises true faith by *fleeing* to Christ for refuge, laying hold on the hope set before him (Heb. 6:18).

True faith embraces Christ in whatever ways the Scriptures hold Him out to poor sinners. The naked soul, destitute of a covering to keep it from the storm of God's wrath, is urged to *"put on"* Christ as a fine raiment (Rom. 13:14).

In whatever way Christ may benefit poor sinners, true faith receives Christ as He holds Himself out in the Scriptures. If He is held out as a *Bridegroom*, true faith comes to Him as a bride. If He is presented as a *Father* (Isa. 9:6), true faith assumes the place of a child. If He is described as a *Shepherd*, true faith takes the place of a sheep. If He is set forth as *Lord*, true faith acknowledges Him to be the *Sovereign*. True faith desires Christ and aspires to be conformed to His image.

It is important to remember, in considering the acts of true saving faith, that not every true believer manifests all these various exercises of faith, for one's condition does not require him to do so. Not everyone in the New Testament is told to sell his possessions (Mark 10:21). Surely, not everyone dares say, "Though He slay me, yet will I trust Him" (Job 13:15). Many would not have pursued Christ like the woman of Canaan (Matt. 15:22–28), but in discouragement would have given up.

There is, however, one thing common to all who possess true saving faith, namely, a heart-satisfaction with God's plan of salvation by Christ. When one is pleased with God's method of satisfying His justice through Christ's person and work and when the soul and heart embrace that plan, then one is believing unto salvation.

Saving faith is not a difficult, mysterious, barely attainable thing. We must first acknowledge it to be God's gift, beyond the power of flesh and blood. God must draw men to Christ. "No one can come to Me unless the Father who sent Me draws him" (John 6:44). "To you it has been granted on behalf of Christ . . . to believe in Him" (Phil. 1:29).

Is faith that consists largely in desire such a mysterious thing? All who have a true appetite for Christ have a mark of true saving faith. "Blessed are those who hunger and thirst for righteousness" (Matt. 5:6). If you will, you are welcome (Rev. 22:17). Is it a matter of such difficulty to look earnestly to the exalted Savior (Isa. 45:22)? Is it mysterious or difficult to receive what is sincerely offered and declared to be mine if I will but accept it? "Open your mouth wide, and I will fill it," says the Lord (Ps. 81:10). Such is justifying faith.

Lordship salvation sees true saving faith as by grace alone. Faith and faith alone is the means of salvation. But such saving faith has certain characteristics and evidences that accompany it. It is more than an inward conviction of the truth-content of the gospel. It is a conviction that involves or results in actions reflecting a genuine inward change. "If anyone is in Christ, he is a new creation; old things have passed away; behold, all things have become new" (2 Cor. 5:17).

Saving Faith Recognizes Who Jesus Is

Nonlordship and lordship teachers differ as to who Jesus is. This, of course, is no secondary matter. Everyone has to be right on this question, or they will not go to heaven. Not that a man has to be perfect in his doctrine or his practice to be a Christian. But there are some truths that every single person—young or old, rich or poor, educated or uneducated—must be right about in order to be a Christian. And the first one is *who Jesus is*.

Matthew Henry, the distinguished Bible commentator, said in his introduction to his exposition of the New Testament, "All the grace contained in this book is owing to Jesus Christ as our Lord and Saviour; and unless we consent to Him as our Lord, we cannot expect any benefit by Him as our Saviour."

Who is Jesus? He is the Lord of Glory—right now. Where is Jesus? He has been exalted to a throne, and He is on that throne right now. "God had sworn with an oath . . . [that] he would raise up the Christ to sit on his throne" (Acts 2:30; see also v. 33). The nonlordship teachers deny that Jesus is reigning now. They teach that His kingship is postponed, and that only later will He sit on His throne. In the same way, they teach that you can have Christ as Savior, and that only later will He become your Lord. Jesus can be your Priest, but for now His prophetic and kingly offices are optional.

But is that what it means to have Christ?

- *Jehovah Witnesses* have a Christ, but not the Christ of the Bible.
- *Mormons* have a Christ, but not the Christ of the Bible.
- *Christian Scientists* have a Christ but not the Christ of the Bible.
- *Unitarians* have a Christ, but not the Christ of the Bible.
- *Liberals* have a Christ, but not the Christ of the Bible.

The nonlordship position has a Christ too, but not the Christ who is Prophet, Priest, and King of His church. By implication, if not by expressed statements, it separates Christ the Priest from Christ the Prophet and King, thus making His lordship optional.

Beyond any doubt or dispute, the fundamental confession of apostolic Christianity was, "Jesus is Lord."

1. *Lordship was the central confession of the whole Christian community.*

> To all who are in Rome, beloved of God, called to be saints: Grace to you and peace from God our Father and the Lord Jesus Christ. (Rom. 1:7)

> To the church of God which is at Corinth, to those who are sanctified in Christ Jesus, called to be saints, with all who in every place call on the name of Jesus Christ our Lord, both theirs and ours. . . . (1 Cor. 1:2)

2. *Lordship was the central confession of the New Testament.*

> Therefore I make known to you that no one speaking by the Spirit of God calls Jesus accursed, and no one can say that Jesus is Lord except by the Holy Spirit. (1 Cor. 12:3)

> For to this end Christ died and rose and lived again, that He might be Lord of both the dead and the living. (Rom. 14:9)

> Therefore God also has highly exalted Him and given Him the name which is above every name, that at the name of Jesus every knee should bow, of those in heaven, and of those on earth, and of those under the earth, and that every tongue should confess that Jesus Christ is Lord, to the glory of God the Father. (Phil 2:9–11)

3. Lordship was the personal confession of New Testament believers.

> And Thomas answered and said to Him, "My Lord and My God!" (John 20:28)

> If you confess with your mouth the Lord Jesus and believe in your heart that God has raised Him from the dead, you will be saved. (Rom. 10:9)

4. Lordship was a key part of presenting the gospel.

> For so an entrance will be supplied to you abundantly into the everlasting kingdom of our Lord and Savior Jesus Christ. (2 Peter 1:11)

> For if, after they have escaped the pollutions of the world through the knowledge of the Lord and Savior Jesus Christ, they are again entangled in them and overcome, the latter end is worse for them than the beginning. (2 Peter 2:20)

> . . . that you may be mindful of the words which were spoken before by the holy prophets, and of the commandment of us the apostles of the Lord and Savior. . . . (2 Peter 3:2)

One of the greatest soul winners that ever lived, Charles Haddon Spurgeon, warned young preachers in his school about this perversion that we see in much evangelism today:

> If the professed convert distinctly and deliberately declares that he knows the Lord's will, but does not mean to attend to it, you are not to pamper his presumptions, but it is your duty to assure him that he is not saved. Do not suppose that the Gospel is magnified or God glorified by going to the worldlings and telling them that they may be saved at this moment

by simply "accepting Christ" as their Saviour, while they are wedded to their idols, and their hearts are still in love with sin. If I do so, I tell them a lie, pervert the Gospel, insult Christ, and turn the grace of God into lasciviousness. It is interesting to notice that the Apostles preached the Lordship of Christ. The word "Saviour" occurs only twice in the Acts of the Apostles (Acts 5:31, 13:23). On the other hand it is amazing to notice the title "Lord" is mentioned 92 times; "Lord Jesus" 13 times; and "The Lord Jesus Christ" 6 times in the same book. The Gospel is "Believe on the Lord Jesus Christ, and thou shalt be saved."

The New Testament statistics should settle the question. Jesus is referred to as "Lord" 822 times, "Lord Jesus" 22 times, and "Lord Jesus Christ" 81 times. The word "Savior" is only used 24 times (eight of which refer to God the Father as our Savior).

If there were no other text in the Bible, Romans 14:9 should erase all doubt as to who Jesus is and why He died and rose: "For to this end Christ died and rose and lived again, that He might be *Lord* both of the dead and the living." When He says, "Come unto me," He does it as the *Lord*. And when He says, "Depart from Me you cursed," He does it as the *Lord*.

It is clear why the champions of the nonlordship gospel say that lordship advocates preach another gospel. They differ as to who Jesus is—and He is the heart of the gospel. When the religious leaders of His day looked Him over carefully, they would not bow to His kingship. Rejecting Him, they did not find salvation. Nor will any one else who will not have Him as Lord.

SIX

Regeneration and Lordship

In this chapter I wish to address the difference between the lordship and the nonlordship views with respect to the doctrine of regeneration. Later, in chapter 10, we shall also consider regeneration, there in reference to the "carnal Christian" teaching.

The lordship and the nonlordship views of regeneration are poles apart, and the differences are many. Without question the best spokesmen of both views would agree that regeneration is absolutely essential for a sinner to be saved— no regeneration, no spiritual life. However, they do not agree on what regeneration is or what it necessarily produces in a person's life.

Regeneration is the key that opens the door of salvation and therefore translates the sinner out of the kingdom of darkness into the kingdom of light. But nonlordship advocates teach a regeneration that does not necessarily transform. Discipleship and obedience are therefore optional, and the biblical fruit of regeneration may or may not be evident. This amounts to a regeneration that does not necessarily regenerate—it does not transform someone into a new creature as described in 2 Corinthians 5:17: "Therefore, if anyone is in

Christ, he is a new creation; old things have passed away; behold all things have become new."

Lordship teaching calls for a regeneration that transforms the whole man—his mind, his affections, and his will. This new birth is a divine miracle and always produces a change in conduct, not just a change of mind. It opens spiritually blind eyes. It unstops spiritually deaf ears. It raises the spiritually dead.

This supernatural change includes revelation. Paul could say, "When it pleased God . . . to reveal His Son in me . . ." (Gal. 1:15, 16). And it produces repentance, faith, humility, and submission. Regeneration in the nonlordship teaching does not necessarily result in the "new creation" described in 2 Corinthians 5:17. Since this verse so vividly describes the results of regeneration, it may be profitable to camp here for a careful look at this vivid and wonderful description of a true Christian.

In Christ

The expression "in Christ" is used 240 times in the New Testament and is the shortest definition of a Christian in the Bible. Indeed, it is the essence of true religion. If I could only ask one question to help a person determine his relationship to his Maker, this would be my question: *Are you in Christ?* Everything God has for you is *in Christ!* "But of Him you are in Christ Jesus, who became for us wisdom from God—and righteousness and sanctification and redemption" (1 Cor. 1:30).

- In Christ is our justification.
- In Christ is our sanctification.
- In Christ is our adoption.
- In Christ is our wisdom.
- In Christ is our righteousness.

"In Christ" signifies a personal relationship. It expresses the most exalted relationship that can exist—an inseparable

52

relationship, an indestructible relationship, an unspeakable relationship that cannot be defined in word only.

New Creation

The second important truth found in this little verse concerns the effects of regeneration: "new creation." Regeneration, (new creation) is the powerful, supernatural work of the Tri-une God. God the Father planned our redemption; God the Son prayed for it (John 17) and purchased it; God the Spirit effectually applies it in regeneration.

We can explain *what* the Spirit does, but *how* He does it let no man pretend to know. "The wind blows where it wishes, and you hear the sound of it, but cannot tell where it comes from and where it goes. So is everyone who is born of the Spirit" (John 3:8). So it is with regeneration.

All Things New

The third important truth found in this precious verse is the evidence of regeneration: "Old things have passed away; behold all things have become new."

How does one know if he or she is regenerate? Regeneration is known by its effects. I have never known a non-lordship teacher to affirm this about regeneration. However, as I noted earlier, true religion cannot be less than

- right thinking in relationship to God—it touches the mind.
- right feeling in relationship to God—it touches the affections.
- right acting in relationship to God—it touches the will.

Regeneration always includes: (1) the enlightening of the mind, (2) the convicting of the conscience, and (3) the renewing of the will. It is by the work of the Spirit that (1) the

natural blindness is removed, (2) the natural enmity is subdued, and (3) the natural man becomes a new creature in all
his views, feelings, desires, affections, aims, habits, and
hopes.

Confusion of Natures

The nonlordship teaching on regeneration does not reflect the
"new creation" described in 2 Corinthians 5:17. Though the
nonlordship view teaches that a new, sinless self is implanted
in the soul, this is something less than regeneration, the new
birth, the rebirth of the old nature. Instead it is the introduction of a new person altogether, a distinct psychological en-
tity. This teaching makes the regeneration experience not a
rebirth of the old soul but the introduction of a new, different soul. This new creature appears to be a part of the divine
nature implanted in the soul. The result is two distinct natures within the Christian. Thus, nothing actually happens to
the old nature. Rather, now there are two side-by-side—the
new and the old.

Lordship teachers hold that in regeneration a new disposition is implanted in the old ego, and thus the Christian
is one person with two struggling principles, but not two distinct natures or selves in one person.

One question nonlordship teachers do not answer is,
How can the old, unchanged, depraved nature on its own exercise faith in Christ? The erroneous nonlordship doctrine of
regeneration also has a profound effect on the doctrine of
progressive sanctification. How can this old, completely unchanged nature yield to the Holy Spirit and become spiritual? Nonlordship teachers have a problem. How can the old
nature—which is really the person—yield to the new nature?
The old nature *cannot* do it because it remains untouched. In
the nonlordship view the old nature is never changed, never
sanctified at all. And the new nature *need not* yield to itself
for it is altogether spiritual. Instead of progressive sanctification, there is a stand-off between the two natures. This

means that a third party, a "third nature," is necessary, to act as a mediator between the old and the new natures and make the critical choices to yield or not to yield to the new nature.

A regeneration that does not regenerate, but only transplants into a person a so-called "new creature" that is not really the same person transformed but something separate from who the person is—this is not regeneration at all!

Nonlordship teachers insist on the necessity of yielding to the Spirit without any real recognition of their theological dilemma—how a totally carnal, unregenerate will can choose to yield. This is just one example of what I stated in chapter 1, that the lordship controversy does not stand alone but affects every major doctrine of Christianity: regeneration, repentance, faith, justification, sanctification, assurance, and our view of the Ten Commandments and their relationship to the gospel.

Old Testament Saints

There is a dispute among nonlordship teachers concerning regeneration and Old Testament saints. For example, Chafer and Walvoord, in *Major Bible Themes* (rev. ed. [Grand Rapids: Zondervan, 1974], 234), do not agree with Dwight Pentecost, who taught that "the fact of the new birth [regeneration] had not been revealed in the Old Testament" (*The Words and Work of Jesus Christ* [Grand Rapids: Zondervan, 1981], 126).

I do not know how Dr. Pentecost would interpret passages like Deuteronomy 30:6: "And the Lord your God will circumcise your heart and the heart of your descendants, to love the Lord your God with all your heart and with all your soul, that you may live"; or Ezekiel 36:26, 27: "I will give you a new heart and put a new spirit within you; I will take the heart of stone out of your flesh and give you a heart of flesh. I will put My Spirit within you and cause you to walk in My statutes, and you will keep My judgments and do them."

Of course the biblical view of regeneration is the supernatural implanting of a new principle, which in turn produces a new principle of conduct, transforming a person and translating him from the kingdom of darkness to the kingdom of light without any intermediate steps. Dispensationalists' views of regeneration have a profound affect on their view of justification and sanctification, and their relationship to each other. (For Chafer's view see his *Systematic Theology*, 6:106.)

Summary

Let me summarize the differences between lordship and nonlordship teachings on the doctrine of regeneration. These summary statements may not represent all nonlordship teachers because they differ among themselves on several details.

A good summary of the lordship definition of regeneration appears in R. C. Sproul's book *Essential Truths of the Christian Faith* (p. 126):

> Regeneration is the theological term used to describe rebirth. It refers to a new generating, a new genesis, a new beginning. It is more than "turning over a new leaf"; it marks the beginning of a new life in a radically renewed person.
>
> Regeneration is the work of the Holy Spirit upon those who are spiritually dead (see Ephesians 2:1–10). The Spirit recreates the human heart, quickening it from spiritual death to spiritual life. Regenerate people are new creations.
>
> Regeneration is not to be confused with the full experience of conversion. Just as birth is our initiation, our first entrance into life outside the womb, so our spiritual rebirth is the starting point of our spiritual life. It occurs by God's divine initiative and is an act that is sovereign, immediate, and instantaneous. An awareness of our conversion may be gradual. Yet rebirth itself is instantaneous. No one can be partially reborn any more than a woman can be partially pregnant.

Regeneration is not the fruit or result of faith. Rather, regeneration precedes faith as the necessary condition for faith. We also do not in any way dispose ourselves toward regeneration or cooperate as co-workers with the Holy Spirit to bring it to pass. We do not decide or choose to be regenerated. God chooses to regenerate us before we will ever choose to embrace Him. To be sure, after we have been regenerated by the sovereign grace of God, we do choose, act, cooperate, and believe in Christ.

One of the fundamental differences between the lordship and nonlordship views is where they place regeneration in the *ordo salutis* (order of salvation). The lordship teaching puts the order of salvation as follows: (1) regeneration, (2) faith and repentance, (3) justification, (4) sanctification (distinct from but always joined to justification), and (5) glorification. Nonlordship teachers have many differences among themselves on the order of salvation. However, I do not know of one leading nonlordship teacher who places regeneration before faith and repentance.

Nonlordship teachers are agreed among themselves that one can experience the new birth and yet not be transformed. The regenerate sinner may turn from his sin or he may not. He may change the direction of his lifestyle or he may not. He may be a disciple or he may not. He may love God and hate sin or he may not.

The lordship view of regeneration is that it is the supernatural work of God whereby the sinner is transformed by the giving of new life in Christ. As a result of this new life the sinner also experiences certain changes. There is deliverance from the dominion of sin and a desire and a power to live a godly life. It is impossible for one to experience regeneration and remain unchanged. Transformation is the clearest evidence of regeneration.

True conversion results in a life that seeks after new obedience and good works. It is unthinkable that one would experience the powerful, supernatural work of regeneration and still have a rebel's heart and live a rebel's life. Certainly the new convert needs to grow in grace and knowledge, but there will be a sincere desire to do so. His affections will be fixed on Jesus—not perfectly but purposefully. Since his will is changed in regeneration, he will now have a desire to obey God despite many failures. His prayer will be "Thy will be done." He will not fall into the ditch of presumption because in front of the ditch of presumption there stands a hedgerow of God's precepts. Nor will he fall into the ditch of despair because in front of the ditch of despair there is a hedgerow of God's promises.

Yes, Christians can and do sin and sometimes grievously. Christians can stumble and fall and they make many crooked steps on their way to the Celestial City. Yes, they can grow cold and they do. Yes, there are failures, sometimes serious failures. Though the winds of temptation and weakness may blow their little ship off course, nevertheless, when the storm subsides they will always get on course again.

The nonlordship teaching on regeneration is that it is the supernatural work of God whereby the sinner is imparted new life, but not necessarily the transformation of life. Changes may take place or they may not take place in the life of the supposed convert. There may be the power of deliverance over authority and dominion of sin or there may not be. There may be the power to live a godly life or there may not be. It is possible to experience regeneration and remain unchanged.

It must be emphasized again that the differences in these two views are not minor. The doctrine of salvation is involved. The two views are as opposite as black and white, as incompatible as oil and water—a fact acknowledged on both sides of the debate. Though both positions are supposedly based on Scripture, one thing is clear—they cannot both be correct interpretations of the Bible.

SEVEN

Repentance and Lordship

One major issue in the lordship controversy is the role of repentance in salvation. Though both the lordship and the non-lordship teachers believe in repentance, they often disagree concerning what the Bible says about it. Their differences on this doctrine have serious implications for other cardinal doctrines of the Christian faith.

When I first read the following statement by Charles Ryrie, I did not know how to react, for it comes from a very respected theologian and able teacher. Referring to lordship preachers, Ryrie wrote in *Balancing the Christian Life* ([Chicago: Moody, 1969], p. 170):

> The importance of this question cannot be overestimated in relation to both salvation and sanctification. The message of faith only and the message of faith plus commitment of life cannot both be the gospel; therefore, one of them is false and comes under the curse of perverting the gospel or preaching another gospel.

This is a serious charge. But is it true? I do not know of one lordship teacher or preacher who denies that sinners are justified by faith alone plus nothing. At the same time, lord-ship teaching emphasizes that faith that is alone is not the kind of faith that justifies. Lordship preachers all believe that biblical repentance and saving faith are inseparably joined to-gether in the application of God's salvation. And as we saw in chapter 5, lordship teachers also recognize that the Bible has much to say about spurious faith, as well as spurious re-pentance.

I find it hard to believe that Charles Ryrie means that such men as Charles H. Spurgeon, John Bunyan, John Gill, John A. Broadus, B. H. Carroll; all the Baptists who embrace the 1689 confession; all the Presbyterians who hold to the Westminster Confession; and all the Christian Reformed be-lievers who hold to the Heidelberg Catechism come "under the curse of perverting the gospel." But as I reflect on his ex-travagant charge, I think Ryrie is partly right—they do preach "another gospel," a different gospel! And if there are two different gospels in this debate, the question that needs to be asked is this: Which one is the biblical gospel? Dr. Ryrie is right about one thing—at stake is the purity of the gospel, as we are about to see further demonstrated in our study on the biblical doctrine of repentance.

The Importance of Repentance

Jesus said, "Unless you repent you will all . . . perish" (Luke 13:3). This warning alone is enough to make repentance of paramount importance. Indeed our Lord made repentance the opening message of His ministry: "Repent, and believe in the gospel" (Mark 1:15). He likewise closed His ministry with a clear command to include repentance in our message to the world: "Repentance and remission of sins should be preached in His name to all nations. . . . and you are wit-nesses of these things" (Luke 24:47–48). He both began and closed His ministry on the subject of repentance.

The renowned Puritan writer and pastor Thomas Wat-son wrote: "Two great graces essential to a saint in this life are faith and repentance. These are the two wings by which he flies to heaven." Repentance is never out of season. If anyone misses repentance, he will miss salvation; he does not have forgiveness of sin and therefore is not in possession of eternal life; he is a lost soul, without God and without hope in this world and the world to come. Jesus Himself tied remission of sins to repentance (Luke 24:47). That makes it very important.

Jesus made repentance His keynote address: "From that time Jesus began to preach and to say, 'Repent, for the kingdom of heaven is at hand'" (Matt. 4:17). The twelve whom He called to preach followed His example: "They went out and preached that people should repent" (Mark 6:12). For example, Peter obeyed our Lord's command to preach repentance and remission of sins. In his first sermon after our Lord returned to heaven Peter said, "Repent, and let every one of you be baptized" (Acts 2:38). Hear Peter again: "Repent . . . and be converted, that your sins may be blotted out" (3:19). In Acts 5:30–32, preaching to his persecutors, he said:

> The God of our fathers raised up Jesus whom you murdered by hanging on a tree. Him God has exalted to His right hand to be Prince and Savior, to give repentance to Israel and forgiveness of sins. And we are His witnesses to these things, and so also is the Holy Spirit whom God has given to those who obey Him.

Our Lord's chief apostle, in his famous sermon on Mars Hill to the Epicurean and Stoic philosophers, preached repentance (Acts 17): "God . . . now commands all men everywhere to repent" (v. 30). Paul, in summarizing a three-year ministry, recounted to the elders of Ephesus just what he had taught and preached: "I kept back nothing that was helpful, but proclaimed it to you, and taught you publicly and from house to house, testifying to Jews, and also to Greeks, repentance toward God and faith toward our Lord Jesus Christ" (Acts 20:20–21).

61

Another example in the life of this great apostle is found in Acts 26. Paul was giving his testimony before King Agrippa, and he told the king what Jesus had told him to do, that is, the purpose for which our Lord had appeared to him. Jesus had said, "I have appeared to you for this purpose, to make you a minister and a witness . . ." (v. 16). In verse 18 the Lord had told Paul that He was sending him to the Gentiles "to open their eyes and to turn them from darkness to light, and from the power of Satan to God, that they may receive forgiveness of sin. . . ." In verse 20, Paul tells King Agrippa the content of the message Jesus gave him: ". . . that they should repent, turn to God, and do works befitting repentance."

Now, this message of repentance almost cost Paul his life. "For these reasons the Jews seized me in the temple and tried to kill me" (v. 21). And one reason preachers avoid preaching repentance is this very point. It will cause some waves of antagonism from this generation of lost, self-deceived church members who are products of evangelism that has left repentance out of its message. Supposed converts, lacking biblical repentance, can become offended when their failure to perform deeds appropriate to repentance is said to evidence a lack of dedication to Christ and His church.

Major Errors of the Nonlordship Position

Nonlordship teachers commit several major errors in their view of repentance.

1. In nonlordship teaching, repentance is not an essential part of salvation.

2. Nonlordship teaching has a forgiveness of sin that is not necessarily joined to repentance.

3. Nonlordship preachers teach that repentance is a call to fellowship with God and has nothing to do with eternal life.

4. Nonlordship teaching removes repentance from any concept of turning from sin initially in coming to faith in Christ.

5. Nonlordship teacher Zane Hodges argues that the word *repentance* is not mentioned in the gospel of John (I will address this later).

6. Nonlordship teaching redefines repentance in such a way as to remove from it any concept of turning from sin. (See, for example, Zane C. Hodges, *Absolutely Free!* [Grand Rapids: Zondervan, 1989], p. 27 and chaps. 9, 12).

7. The nonlordship position argues that regeneration does not necessarily produce faith and repentance. Robert Lightner says that "repentance is *almost* a synonym for faith" (*The Savior, Sin, and Salvation* [Nashville: Nelson, 1991], p. 167). Though Lightner is the most skillful writer for the nonlordship position, he is like a good lawyer with a bad case. Statements such as this clearly show that he does not believe regeneration always precedes faith and repentance; and if it does not precede them, it does not produce them. The nonlordship teaching denies that there is an inseparable connection between faith and repentance. This inseparable relationship warrants full consideration. What God has joined together let no man put asunder.

Other nonlordship teachers goes so far as to say:

- "Any teaching that demands a change of conduct toward either God or man for salvation is to add works or human effort to faith, and this contradicts all Scripture and is an accursed message."
- "Lordship salvation contradicts Scripture."
- "This message is accursed of God."
- "The person who preaches such a message [lordship] is also accursed of God."

These quotations come from Stanford, Seymore, and Streib, *Handbook of Personal Evangelism* (Hollywood, Fla.: Florida Bible College, 1975), 91–95. They reflect antinomianism at its worst.

Zane Hodges also separates faith and repentance in his book *Absolutely Free!* when he says, "Faith alone (not repentance and faith) is the sole condition for justification and eternal life" (p. 144). Noting that when the Philippian jailor asked Paul and Silas, "What must I do to be saved?" they answered, "Believe on the Lord Jesus Christ, and you will be saved" (Acts 16:30–31), Hodges argues: "There is not a word here—not a syllable—about repentance. Lordship salvation teachers are in dire straits with a text like this" (p. 144).

Hodges seeks support for his case in Calvin's *Institutes*, book 3, chapter 3. However, he apparently has not read Calvin carefully, because the Reformer's words destroy his arguments. Calvin says in that chapter, "With good reason, the sum of the gospel is held to consist in repentance and forgiveness of sins (Luke 24:47; Acts 5:31)"; and "surely no one can embrace the grace of the gospel without betaking himself from the errors of his past life into the right way, applying his whole effort to the practice of repentance" (*Institutes*, 3.3.1). Further, he says, "Repentance has its foundation in the gospel, which faith embraces" (3.3.2). A little later Calvin asks: "What then? Can true repentance stand, apart from faith? Not at all. But even though they cannot be separated, they ought to be distinguished. As faith is not without hope, yet faith and hope are different things, so repentance and faith, although they are held together by a permanent bond, required to be joined rather than confused" (3.3.5).

Faith and Repentance Are Inseparable

At the beginning of His Galilean ministry Jesus said: "The time is fulfilled, and the kingdom of God is at hand. Repent, and believe in the gospel" (Mark 1:15). Note the twofold command—in God's salvation *faith and repentance* are inseparable.

If repentance is only a change of mind, how do I know I have changed my mind? Do I just say I have changed my mind? One can only be sure that he has changed his mind if that changed mind leads to change in his direction. Just as regeneration can only be known in its effects on the life, a changed mind can only be known by a changed direction.

True repentance is always consistent with true faith. Spurious repentance dwells on the consequences of sin rather than on sin itself. I have known some sinners so disturbed with the fears of hell and thoughts of death and eternal judgment that, to use the words of one old preacher, "They have been shaking over the mouth of hell by their collar, and have almost felt the torments of the pit before they went there." Such fears may come with true repentance, but they are not the essential part of repentance. As John Bunyan, in his *Holy War*, has well said, "Diabolus often beats the great hell-drum in the ears of Mansoul, to prevent their hearing the trumpet of the gospel which proclaims mercy and pardon."

Any repentance that keeps a sinner from believing in Christ is a repentance that needs to be repented of. Any repentance that makes a sinner think Christ will not save him goes beyond the truth of the Bible; yes, it goes against the truth. Any repentance that leads to despair and remorse but does not embrace mercy is a repentance of the Devil and not of God.

A person may feel he has done wrong but go on sinning all the same, feeling that there is no hope and that he may as well continue seeking the pleasures of sin since he cannot, so he thinks, have the pleasures of grace and forgiveness. That is spurious repentance. It is the fire of the Devil, which hardens the heart in sin, and not the Lord's fire of mercy, which melts the heart in repentance. In Peter's repentance he wept bitterly yet embraced the mercy of God in Christ. One old Puritan, on his sick bed, expressed it this way: "Lord, sink me low as hell in repentance; but lift me high as heaven in faith."

To express it yet another way, true repentance is to sorrow bitterly for sin you know should damn you but rejoice greatly in Christ as if the sin were nothing at all.

What is true evangelical repentance? Why do I say "evangelical"? Because there is also a legal repentance. What is the difference? Legal repentance does not embrace the mercy of Christ. Consider Judas (Matt. 27:3). He repented—he was remorseful. But his was not evangelical repentance.

We see the two aspects of repentance—grief over sin and turning from sin—in our definition of repentance taken from the Westminster Shorter Catechism.

> Q. 87. *What is repentance unto life?*
> A. Repentance unto life is a saving grace, whereby a sinner, out of a true sense of his sin, and apprehension of the mercy of God in Christ, doth, with grief and hatred of his sin, turn from it unto God, with full purpose of, and endeavor after, new obedience.

Notice the phrase, "and apprehension of the mercy of God in Christ." One might think it strange that grasping "the mercy of God in Christ" is a defining feature of repentance. But it only underscores the point that where saving faith is found, there evangelical repentance will be found also, and where evangelical repentance is found, there true saving faith will be found. They are Siamese twins—inseparable on arrival.

Repentance strips a person of self-righteousness, and faith clothes him with Christ. Repentance purges the soul of dead works, and faith fills the soul with living works. Repentance pulls down, and faith builds up. Repentance orders a time to weep, and faith gives a time to dance. Together these two make up the work of grace within, whereby men's souls are saved.

The repentance we ought to preach is one connected with faith. Thus we may preach repentance and faith together without any difficulty whatsoever. Like twins, they are born at the same time. To say which is first is beyond my knowledge. They come to the soul together, and we must preach them together.

Spurgeon said, "So then, dear friends, those people who have faith which allows them to think lightly of past sin, have the faith of devils and not the faith of God's elect."

Our need to repent and believe continues until our dying day. Rowland Hill, when he was near death, said he had one regret, and that was that a dear friend who lived with him for sixty years would have to leave him at the gate of heaven. "That dear friend, said he, is repentance; repentance has been with me all my life, and I think I shall drop a tear, said the good man, as I go through the gates to think that I can repent no more."

Repentance in the Gospel of John

As mentioned earlier, Zane C. Hodges makes much of the fact that the gospel of John does not use the word *repent*. What Hodges fails to recognize is that the word itself does not need to appear for us to see the principle of repentance as part of the message of God-centered evangelism.

Let me illustrate from our Lord's evangelism. In Jesus' encounter with the rich young ruler (Mark 10:17–22), the young man wanted to know what to do to have eternal life (v. 17). The Master Evangelist addressed the young ruler's question without mentioning the word *believe* or *repent*. Nonetheless, Jesus got to the heart of the issue of true repentance and saving faith by showing the young man that he could not have two Gods and that, therefore, he must turn from what we might call his "green god." "Then Jesus, looking at him, loved him, and said to him, 'One thing you lack: Go your way, sell whatever you have and give to the poor, and you will have treasures in heaven; and come, take up the cross, and follow Me'" (v. 21). This is preaching repentance, and it was necessary for the rich young ruler to turn *from*, as well as *to*, in order to have eternal life.

Jesus taught repentance in John 8 when He told the harlot to "sin no more" (v. 11), that is, turn from sin. It is not necessary to use the word *repent* to teach repentance. The word *repent* was not used in the parable of the prodigal son (Luke 15:11–32), but he did repent—he turned from his sin and embraced his father's mercy.

Summarizing True Repentance

First Thessalonians 1:9 sets forth three things that happen in every true conversion to some degree: "For they themselves declare concerning us what manner of entry we had to you, and how you turned to God from idols to serve the living and true God." Paul says that the Thessalonians

1. turned to God (faith);
2. turned from idols (from sin—repentance);
3. to serve ("do works meet for repentance"—evidence of repentance).

At the center of these three responses, and inseparable from faith and good works, is repentance. Repentance and faith are sacred duties and inseparable graces wrought in our souls by the regenerating Spirit of God, whereby being deeply convicted of our guilt, danger, and helplessness, and of the way of salvation by Christ, we turn to God with unfeigned contrition, confession, and supplication for mercy; at the same time heartily receiving the Lord Jesus Christ as our Prophet, Priest, and King, and relying on Him alone as the only and all-sufficient Savior.

From this summary, we see that:

1. The seat of true repentance is in the soul. It is not of itself a mere intellectual knowledge of sin, or the sorrow that accompanies it, or the changed life that flows from it, but it is the soul's apprehension of its heinous character, which produces the horror and self-loathing that accompany it, and the determination to forsake sin that flows from it.
2. True repentance is inconsistent with the continuance in sin because of abounding grace.
3. True repentance consists of mental and spiritual emotion, and not of outward self-imposed chastisements.

Even the pious life and devotion to God that follow are described not as repentance, but as fruits meet for repentance.

The Second London Baptist Confession of 1689 contains an excellent summary explanation of repentance in chapter 15, reproduced in its entirety below:

OF REPENTANCE UNTO LIFE AND SALVATION

1. Such of the elect as are converted at riper years, having sometimes lived in the state of nature, and therein served divers lusts and pleasures, God in their effectual calling giveth them repentance unto life.

2. Whereas there is none that doth good and sinneth not, and the best of men may, through the power and deceitfulness of their corruption dwelling in them, with the prevalency of temptation, fall in to great sin and provocations; God hath, in the covenant of grace, mercifully provided that believers so sinning and falling be renewed through repentance unto salvation.

3. This saving repentance is an evangelical grace, whereby a person, being by the Holy Spirit made sensible of the manifold evils of his sin, doth, by faith in Christ, humble himself for it with godly sorrow, detestation of it, and self-abhorrency, praying for pardon and strength of grace, with the purpose and endeavor, by supplies of the Spirit, to walk before God unto all well-pleasing in all things.

4. As repentance is to be continued through the whole course of our lives, upon the account of the body of death, and the motions thereof, so it is every man's duty to repent of his particular known sins particularly.

5. Such is the provision which God hath made through Christ in the covenant of grace for the preser-

vation of believers unto salvation, that although there is no sin so small but it deserves damnation, yet there is no sin so great that it shall bring damnation on them that repent, which makes the constant preaching of repentance necessary.

EIGHT

Justification and Sanctification

In chapter 7 we considered some of the major differences between lordship and nonlordship views of repentance. In this chapter we will be considering some of the important differences in respect to the doctrine of sanctification and its inseparable relationship to justification. (Though they cannot be separated, they must be distinguished.)

Justification and sanctification are two vitally important doctrines of the Christian faith, as a visit to any communion service should prove.

The New Covenant

Every time we observe the Lord's Supper we are brought face to face with justification and sanctification. In any communion service the minister refers to one or more of the following passages of Scripture, all of which speak of the new covenant.

- "And He took the cup, and gave thanks, and gave it to them, saying, 'Drink from it, all of you. For this is

My blood of the new covenant, which is shed for many for the remission of sins'" (Matt. 26:27–28).
- "And He said to them, 'This is My blood of the new covenant, which is shed for many'" (Mark 14:24).
- "Likewise He also took the cup after supper, saying, 'This cup is the new covenant in My blood, which is shed for you'" (Luke 22:20).
- "In the same way He also took the cup after supper, saying, 'This cup is the new covenant in My blood. This do, as often as you drink it, in remembrance of Me'" (1 Cor. 11:25).

What is the new covenant? If you do not know, then these passages will not make sense to you. Thousands of preachers all over the world hold a little cup of grape juice or wine before their congregations and say, "This cup is the new covenant in My blood"; but many of those to whom those words are spoken have no idea of what the new covenant is.

According to Spurgeon, "The covenant is the marrow of divinity." Perhaps you are thinking: *Is that all so important? We know that the juice symbolizes the blood of Christ.* Let me underscore just how important that covenant really is.

- Hebrews 12:24 refers to "Jesus the Mediator of the new covenant."
- Second Corinthians 3:6 speaks of able "ministers of the new covenant."
- Matthew 26:28 teaches us that forgiveness of sins is bound up with the new covenant: "This is My blood of the new covenant, which is shed for many for the remission of sins."

In other words:

- What Christ purchased as "Mediator of the new covenant" were the benefits and blessings of the new covenant.

72

- What the apostles preached concerning Christ as able "ministers of the new covenant" was the gospel of the new covenant.
- The salvation sinners received, when they were called by the Spirit, included the benefits and blessings of the new covenant.

Just what are those benefits and blessings of the new covenant? They are the two greatest and most essential blessings of the gospel. In fact, all of the many other blessings of Christianity flow from these two foundational blessings.

The Two Greatest Problems

In order to appreciate these two foundational blessings, let us first address the question, What are man's two greatest problems? Some might say, "My greatest problem is my husband," "my wife," "my children," "my parents," "my school teacher," "my health," "my finances," or " my environment."
No! You have two greater problems. What are they?

- A bad record in heaven because of your sinful thoughts, words, and deeds.
- A bad heart on earth, which produces the sins that cause the bad record in heaven.

Jeremiah, in his prophecy of the new covenant, points out the answer to these two problems: "I will make a new covenant . . . I will put My law in their minds, and write it on their hearts [a changed heart]. . . . I will forgive their iniquity, and their sin I will remember no more [a new record]" (Jer. 31:31–34). Hebrews 10:16–17 underscores these two promises: "This is the covenant that I will make with them after those days, says the Lord: I will put My laws into their hearts, and in their minds I will write them . . . their sins and their lawless deeds I will remember no more" (see also Heb. 8:10–12).

All of man's problems have their beginning in these two: a bad record in heaven and a bad heart on earth. What, then, are the two basic blessings of the new covenant?

- A changed record in heaven by the blood of Christ—justification.
- A new heart on earth by the power of the Spirit—the beginning of sanctification.

The new covenant is one covenant with two inseparable aspects. Bound up in the covenant are these two central doctrines on the Christian faith—justification and sanctification.

The Relationship of Justification to Sanctification

The following truth cannot be overemphasized: The working of God's Spirit in our hearts on earth and the cleansing of our sins by Christ's blood in heaven are inseparably joined together in the application of God's salvation. Justification and sanctification always go together in salvation. Any attempt to place the basic act of submission to Christ after conversion cuts the vital nerve of the new covenant and perverts biblical Christianity. To separate these blessings which God has joined together in one covenant is to bring dishonor on the blood that was shed to enact the entirety of the new covenant.

How I wish everyone who heard the words "This is My blood of the new covenant" would know, experience, and understand the blessings and benefits of that covenant! Then all would realize that there is no justification without sanctification, no forgiveness without growth in grace, no new standing with God without a new walk with God, no having Jesus as Savior without also having Him as Lord!

The nonlordship teachers do not agree that justification and sanctification, though distinguishable doctrines, are inseparably joined together in the application of God's salvation. They make sanctification optional; a justified person may or may not be sanctified. They would not concur with Robert Murray M'Cheyne when he said of the gospel:

> It is a holy making gospel. Without holy fruits all evidences are vain. Dear friends, you have awakenings, enlightenings, experiences, and many due signs; but if you lack holiness, you shall never see the Lord. A real desire after complete holiness is the truest mark of being born again. Jesus is a holy Saviour. He first covers the soul with His white raiment then makes the soul glorious—restores the lost image of God, and fills the soul with pure, heavenly holiness. Unregenerate men among you cannot bear this testimony.

If God ever gives you salvation, be sure holiness will be a part of it. If Christ does not wash you from the filth of sin, you have no part with Him. Jesus said to Peter, "If I do not wash you, you have no part with Me" (John 13:8). It is a strange kind of salvation that does not have a desire after purity and holiness. Such a salvation was never purchased by the blood of Christ. "He will save His people from their sins" (Matt. 1:21)—not *in* their sins, but *from* their sins.

The Puritan Thomas Adams said, "They know not Christ who seek to divide His blood from His water, and they shall fail in justification in heaven that refuse sanctification on earth."

There are many reasons why this truth should concern every serious Christian.

- It involves true conversion.
- It bears directly on the many self-deceived church members who have walked aisles, troubled baptismal waters, signed decision cards, and had their names entered on church rolls, yet who give no biblical evidence of Holy Ghost regeneration. Can a serious person look at present-day church members and not be moved with holy concern and compassion?

75

- It puts repentance back into the evangelistic message.
- It deals a death blow to all second-work-of-grace teachings, such as the "higher life," the "crucified life," and the "deeper life," which represent a wrong view of sanctification—"let go and let God."
- It should settle the lordship controversy by putting to rest the notion that Jesus as Savior is little more than a hell insurance policy, and that obedience is optional.

Charles Ryrie, in his book *So Great Salvation* (Wheaton, Ill.: Victor, 1989), says: "But what of sanctification? Nowhere does it appear in Paul's list in Romans 8:29, 30—only predestination, calling, justification and glorification—why is sanctification not included? Could it be that Paul did not want to base our guarantee, our ultimate glorification on our sanctification?" (p. 150).

This is a commentary on the nonlordship view of the relationship between justification and sanctification. What if we were to apply his reasoning to 1 Corinthians 1:30: "But of Him are you in Christ Jesus, who became for us wisdom from God—and righteousness and sanctification and redemption"? There justification is not mentioned. Why? It is understood to be inseparably joined to sanctification. Likewise, in Romans 8:29–30 justification is mentioned but sanctification is not. Why? Because where justification is, there sanctification will be also. It is the same with faith and repentance. Where there is true belief, there will always be evangelical repentance, and where true repentance is found, there will always be saving faith.

The serious error of the nonlordship teaching is that it does not see that justification and sanctification, like faith and repentance, are inseparably joined in the application of God's salvation. Justification and sanctification will always be present in a true Christian. The Bible knows nothing about a justified man in whom sanctification has not begun. Nor does the Bible know anything of a sanctified man who has not been justified.

The Bible says that without holiness (sanctification) no man will see the Lord (Heb. 12:14). This refers not to a positional sanctification, which every believer possesses once for all. The passage is referring to personal holiness that every believer is duty-bound to pursue continually.

Let me put it one more way: no one will attain to a right standing before God by pursuing holiness. Likewise, none who fails to pursue holiness will see God's face in peace. Please note, I say "pursue." Only One has attained absolute holiness—Jesus alone was perfect.

Let me emphasize again that although justification and sanctification cannot be separated in the application of God's salvation, they must be distinguished. As faith is not without hope but the two are held together by a permanent bond, joined rather than confused, so it is with justification and sanctification. Though distinct, they must be held together by a permanent bond.

In nonlordship teaching, repentance and sanctification are not necessarily parts of God's salvation. Such teaching is not only out of step with historic Christianity but also out of step with the analogy of faith and the analogy of Scripture—the rule of interpretation, that Scripture is the best interpreter of Scripture, and that biblical truths and passages do not conflict with each other.

The Westminster Larger Catechism is most helpful at expressing the distinct yet harmonious relationship between justification and sanctification:

Q. 77. *Wherein do justification and sanctification differ?*

A. Although sanctification be inseparably joined with justification, yet they differ, in that God in justification imputeth the righteousness of Christ; in sanctification his Spirit infuseth grace, and enableth to the exercise thereof; in the former, sin is pardoned; in the other, it is subdued; the one doth equally free all believers from the revenging wrath of God, and that perfectly in this life, that they never fall into condemnation; the other is neither equal in all, nor in this life perfect in any, but growing up to perfection.

I close this chapter with the words of the prince of the Puritans, John Owen (from *Works of John Owen* [Edinburgh: Banner of Truth, 1965], 3:370):

There is mention in the Scripture of a two-fold sanctification, and consequently of a two-fold holiness. The first is common unto persons and things, consisting of the peculiar dedication, consecration, or separation of them unto the service of God, by His own appointment, whereby they become holy. Thus the priests and Levites of old, the ark, the altar, the tabernacle, and the temple, were sanctified and made holy; and, indeed, in all holiness whatever, there is a peculiar dedication and separation unto God. But in the sense mentioned, this was solitary and alone. No more belonged unto it but this sacred separation, nor was there any other effect of this sanctification. But, secondly, there is another kind of sanctification and holiness, wherein this separation to God is not the first thing done or intended, but a consequent and effect thereof. This is real and eternal, by the communicating of a principle of holiness unto our natures, attended with its exercise in acts and duties of holy obedience to the holy law of God.

NINE

The "Carnal Christian" Teaching, 1— Two Classes of Christian?

Another major theological difference between lordship and nonlordship theologies concerns the "carnal Christian" theory. This theory is one of the most perverse teachings in our generation. It is so dangerous and self-deceiving that in many cases it is damning. As a result of this erroneous teaching many who regularly occupy our church pews on Sunday mornings and fill our church rolls are strangers to true conversion—strangers to heart religion—because they have never experienced the power of a changed life. They are not new creatures in whom old things have passed away (2 Cor. 5:17).

The "carnal Christian" teaching was invented to accommodate all the supposed converts of modern evangelism, which has left biblical repentance out of its message. I am referring to those who make "decisions," walk aisles, and profess to being Christians while their lives remain unchanged by the power of the Holy Spirit. They are people who do not love what Christians love or hate what Christians hate. Because these supposed converts think and behave like non-Christians, their teachers have devised an explanation for their unchanged lives; they have invented the unbiblical category of "carnal Christian."

The "carnal Christian" idea is part of the nonlordship two-experience theory of the Christian life. Stage one is conversion, the decision to receive Christ as one's personal Savior (and thus escape hell). Stage two, a later decision, makes Christ Lord. (Nonlordship teachers seem to ignore the fact that no human being makes Christ Lord. He is Lord by God Almighty's decree, regardless of what sinners say, think, or do. "Therefore let all the house of Israel know assuredly that God has made this Jesus, whom you crucified, both Lord and Christ" [Acts 2:36]. This verse should settle the question of who makes Christ Lord.)

Between these two stages or experiences, the supposed convert may live like a non-Christian. A testimony would sound something like this: "When I was seven or eight years old, I received Christ as my personal Savior, but I did not make Him Lord until much later in life." As we saw in chapter 2, such a testimony reflects an erroneous interpretation of experience. That is why we must always interpret our experiences by the Scripture and never interpret the Scripture by our experiences.

The notion of two kinds of Christians is just the old "second blessing" teaching in new garb—a teaching that sends Christians on a quest for an instantaneous holiness that does not exist.

Hebrews 13:9 warns us, "Do not be carried about with various and strange doctrines." The New English Bible puts it like this: "So don't be swept off your course by all sorts of outlandish teaching." The Living Bible paraphrase reads, "So do not be attracted by strange, new ideas." The "carnal Christian" doctrine is indeed a "strange" and "outlandish" teaching, based on an erroneous interpretation of a single passage of Scripture (1 Cor. 3:1–4, which we will examine later). There is reason to believe that this theory has spawned the terrible perversion of the gospel known as nonlordship salvation.

I write on this very serious issue with deep feelings of sorrow and apprehension. Why? The teaching that I wish to expose is held by many fine Christians and taught by many able and respected teachers. This fact causes me to approach the subject with much concern and with great caution. For many years I myself espoused and taught the "carnal Christian" error. The Lord had mercy on me!

It bears repeating here what we observed in chapter 2, that a Christian's experience with God may be better than his understanding of divine truth. His formulation of doctrines may be tainted with error and ignorance. The opposite may also be true; that is, a person's intellectual understanding may be good, but his experience faulty. The church of Sardis, for example, had a reputation for being alive—subscribing to the truth—but in experience they were dead (Rev. 3:1).

My motive, purpose, and prayer in this chapter and the next is to promote true understanding, holiness, and usefulness among Christians, in place of a most dangerous and debilitating doctrine.

Popular Sources of "Carnal Christian" Teaching

The idea of two categories of Christians has been popularized by the *Scofield Reference Bible,* Dallas Theological Seminary, and Campus Crusade for Christ. Scofield wrote that

> Paul divides men into three classes: "Natural" i.e. the Adamic Man, unrenewed through the new birth; "Spiritual" i.e. the renewed man as Spirit-filled and walking in the Spirit in full communion with God; "Carnal", "fleshly", i.e. the renewed man who walking "after the flesh", remains a babe in Christ. (pp. 1213–14)

Notice two very important points in this Scofield note: (1) the division of humanity into three classes; (2) the description of one class as "carnal," "fleshly," "babe(s) in Christ," "who walk after the flesh." "Walk" implies the bent

81

of their lives; their leaning or bias is in the direction of carnality.

One of the most popular presentations of this view is a small tract, which explains, "After you have invited Christ to come into your life, it is possible for you to take control of the throne of your life again." First Corinthians 2:14–3:3 is thought to identify three kinds of people, as illustrated below:

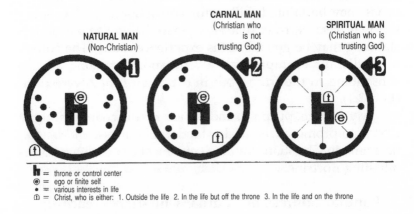

The first circle accurately enough represents the non-Christian. Note the position of the ego, indicating that self is on the throne. The natural man is self-centered. His interests are controlled by self. The cross is outside the person's life.

Now compare that with the second circle, where the only difference is that a cross (representing Christ) appears inside, but not on the throne. The ego is still on the throne, indicating that there has been no basic change in the person's nature and character. That is to say, the bent of the life of the "carnal Christian" is the same as that of the non-Christian. Circle two gives basically the same picture as circle one, the only difference being that the "carnal Christian" has made a profession of receiving Jesus into his life. But he is not trusting God.

A brief examination of this diagram and its interpretation of 1 Corinthians 3:1–4 will show that it illustrates the view we have already found in the Scofield Bible notes. We ought not to miss three very salient and important facts about the teaching:

First, we note again that it divides all men into three classes or categories. With this fact none of its proponents disagree, though they may present and apply it differently.

Second, one class or category is set out as containing the "Christian" who "walks after the flesh." The center of his life is self, and he is the same as the unrenewed man as far as the bent of his life is concerned.

Third, all those who accept this view use 1 Corinthians 3:1–4 to support their position. If it can be established that the preponderance of Scripture teaches only two classes or categories of men—regenerate and unregenerate, converted and unconverted, those in Christ and those outside of Christ—that should weigh heavily against the "carnal Christian" interpretation of 1 Corinthians 3:1–4.

Before I turn to some of the errors and dangers of the "carnal Christian" teaching, it may be wise to clarify what I am *not* saying. I am not overlooking the biblical teaching about sin in the Christian life, about babes in Christ, about growth in grace, about Christians who backslide grievously, and about the divine chastisement that Christians receive.

I acknowledge that there are babes in Christ. In fact there are not only babes in Christ but different stages of "babyhood" in terms of understanding divine truth and spiritual growth. I also recognize that there is a sense in which Christians may be said to be carnal, but I must add that there are different degrees of carnality. Every Christian is carnal in some area of his life at many times in his life—"the flesh lusts against the Spirit" (Gal. 5:17).

Not all the marks of Christianity are equally apparent in all Christians. Nor are these marks manifest to the same degree in every period of a Christian's life. Love, faith, obedience, and devotion will vary in the same Christian at different stages of his Christian experience. In other words, there are many degrees of sanctification.

Moreover, the Christian's progress in growth is not constant and undisturbed. There are many hills and valleys in the process of sanctification—many stumblings and crooked steps on the pathway to the Celestial City. The Bible offers examples of grievous falls and carnality in the lives of true believers. Thus we have the warnings of temporal judgment and of chastisement by our heavenly Father.

These truths we all acknowledge, and they are not the point of this study. The question we have to consider is, Does the Bible divide Christians into two exclusive categories, one spiritual and the other carnal? This is the issue at the heart of the "carnal Christian" teaching.

Errors in the "Carnal Christian" Teaching

Error #1: The misuse of 1 Corinthians 3. The "carnal Christian" doctrine wrongly interprets and applies the sole passage of Scripture on which it is based, 1 Corinthians 3:1–4. (The historical and true interpretation will be dealt with later in this chapter.)

The most doctrinal portion of the New Testament is Paul's letter to the Romans, as all reasonable Bible scholars and theologians would agree. Most would further agree that Paul's letter to the Galatians is the second most doctrinal portion of the New Testament. The first letter to the church at Corinth deals primarily with practical problems in the church:

chapters 1–3   Strife and contentions about the ministers (see 1:12–13; 3:3–6; 3:21–22)

chapter 5   Immorality and incest (v. 1); lack of repentance (v. 2)

6:1–10   Lawsuits against one another (v. 7); defrauding and wronging one another (v. 8)

7:1–17   Sexuality in marriage: instruction that sex was for more than procreation

8:1–13   Christian liberty; weak and strong Christians; fighting over meat offered to idols

84

In all of these concerns there was the danger of carnal behavior among Christians. For example, those who fell into strife, division, and contentions over ministers in chapters 1–3 were carnal, resembling the unregenerate, in that particular respect. Chapter 3 does not speak of three categories of mankind or two classes of Christians, but of carnal versus spiritual attitudes and behaviors. That should be clear from the rest of the Bible.

The following two doctrinal passages are only two of many Scriptures that clearly teach that all mankind is divided into two categories and no more:

There is therefore now no condemnation to those who are in Christ Jesus, who do not walk according to the flesh, but according to the Spirit. For the law of the Spirit of life in Christ Jesus has made me free from the law of sin and death. For what the law could not do in that it was weak through the flesh, God did by sending His own Son in the likeness of sinful flesh, on account of sin: He condemned sin in the flesh, that the righteous requirement of the law might be fulfilled in us who do not walk according to the flesh but according to the Spirit. For those who live according to the flesh set their minds on the things of the flesh, but those who live according to the Spirit, the things of the Spirit. For to be carnally minded is death, but to be

spiritually minded is life and peace. Because the carnal mind is enmity against God; for it is not subject to
the law of God, nor indeed can it be. So then, those
who are in the flesh cannot please God. But you are
not in the flesh but in the Spirit, if indeed the Spirit of
God dwells in you. Now if anyone does not have the
Spirit of Christ, he is not His. (Rom. 8:1–9)

For the flesh lusts against the Spirit, and the Spirit
against the flesh; and these are contrary to one another,
so that you do not do the things that you wish. But if
you are led by the Spirit, you are not under the law.
Now the works of the flesh are evident, which are:
adultery, fornication, uncleanness, licentiousness, idolatry, sorcery, hatred, contentions, jealousies, outbursts
of wrath, selfish ambitions, dissensions, heresies, envy,
murders, drunkenness, revelries, and the like; of which
I tell you beforehand, just as I also told you in time
past, that those who practice such things will not in-
herit the kingdom of God. But the fruit of the Spirit is
love, joy, peace, longsuffering, kindness, goodness,
faithfulness, gentleness, self-control. Against such there
is no law. And those who are Christ's have crucified
the flesh with its passions and desires. (Gal. 5:17–24)

These two passages set out what the rest of the Bible
clearly teaches, namely, that there are only two classes or categories of people, within which there may be many shades
and degrees. To interpret 1 Corinthians 3:1–4 in such a way
as to divide humanity into three classes is, therefore, to vio-
late the cardinal rules of biblical interpretation: interpret single passages in the light of the whole of Scripture; interpret
all subordinate passages in the light of the leading truths; interpret all obscure passages in the light of clear passages.

The "carnal Christian" teaching fails to do that. It is an
incorrect interpretation and application of the one portion of
Scripture on which it is founded.

Error #2: Separating the blessings of the new covenant. The "carnal Christian" teaching distorts the two basic blessings of the new covenant—justification and sanctification—and their relationship to each other. Justification is what Christ does *for* us in heaven; He covers our record with His blood and gives us a legal right to enter in. Sanctification is what Christ does *in* us by His Holy Spirit on earth—this gives us a measure of practical fitness for heaven.

The working of His Spirit in us and His cleansing us by His blood are inseparably joined in the application of His grace. Any attempt to place the act of submission subsequent to conversion cuts the living nerve out of the new covenant. The "carnal Christian" teaching does just that. It separates what God has joined together and thus perverts biblical Christianity, bringing dishonor on the blood of Christ shed to enact the entirety of the new covenant—both justification and sanctification.

The *Catechism for Young Children* sums it up beautifully:

> Q. 49. *What did God the Father undertake in the covenant of grace?*
> A. To justify and sanctify those for whom Christ should die.

"For you" is your creed. *"In* you" is your experience.

Error #3: Mistaking spurious faith for saving faith. The "carnal Christian" teaching does not distinguish between true, saving belief and spurious belief, a distinction made in the following Scriptures:

- "Many believed in His name. . . . But Jesus did not commit Himself to them" (John 2:23–24).
- "Many believed in Him but . . . did not confess Him" (John 12:42).
- "[Some] believe for a while and in time of temptation fall away" (Luke 8:13).

- "Simon [Magus] also believed . . . was baptized" (Acts 8:13); but he thought he could buy the Holy Spirit. Peter said he would "perish" (v. 20); his heart was "not right" (v. 21); unchanged, he was "poisoned by bitterness and bound by iniquity" (v. 23). But the strongest evidence of his spurious faith was in his prayer. Like the unregenerate, he was only concerned with the consequence of sin, "that none of these things . . . come upon me" (v. 24). He made no request to be pardoned and cleansed from his sin.
- "The devils believe . . ." (James 2:19).

In all of these cases there was belief, that is, faith; but it was not saving faith. Likewise all "carnal Christians" have belief, but it is not always saving belief (see chap. 5, on saving faith).

Error #4: The omission of repentance. The "carnal Christian" teaching excludes repentance, at least by implication, in that someone who lives and acts just like the natural man may still be regarded as a Christian. This is easily seen in the diagram in which the self is still on the throne. Failure to teach the necessity of repentance is a very grave error and a departure from the apostolic example of gospel proclamation (see chap. 7, on repentance).

Error #5: A wrong view of assurance. The "carnal Christian" teaching ignores much biblical teaching on the doctrine of assurance, particularly that Christian character and conduct have much to do with assurance. (For the lordship view of assurance see the Baptist Confession of 1689, chap. 18.) I will have more on assurance in a later chapter.

Questions Arising Out of the "Carnal Christian" Teaching

The following are several questions concerning the implications of "carnal Christian" teaching.

88

1. Are believers sanctified passively, that is, by faith without the deeds of the law? (Note well, I did not say "justified" but "sanctified.") If sanctification is passive—a kind of "let go and let God" experience—then what do we make of the apostolic expressions in the New Testament such as "I fight," "I run," "I keep under my body," "let us cleanse ourselves," "let us labor," "let us lay aside every weight," etc.?

2. Does not appealing to the so-called "carnal Christian" to become a spiritual Christian depreciate the real conversion experience by making necessary a second experience, variously described as the "higher life," the "deeper life," the "Spirit-filled life," "triumphant living," and "making Christ Lord"?

3. Has the spiritual Christian finished growing in grace? If not, what is he to be called as he continues to grow in grace? Ought we to make still more unbiblical categories, such as, the "spiritual-spiritual Christian" or the "super-spiritual Christian"?

4. Who is to decide who the "carnal Christians" are, and exactly what standard is to be used in determining this? Do the spiritual Christians decide who the "carnal Christians" are? Does a church or preacher decide where the line is to be drawn between the two classes or categories? Would you like the responsibility of dividing the members of your church into unsaved, "carnal Christian," and spiritual? Since all Christians have remaining sin in them and since they sin every day, how much sin or what particular sins warrant that a person be classified a "carnal Christian"?

5. Do not all Christians act like natural men at times and in some area of their lives?

6. Do not inward sins such as envy, malice, covetousness, lasciviousness (which includes immorality on the mental level) prove that a person is in some degree carnal as much as do external sins?

7. How much sin can a spiritual Christian commit and still remain in the spiritual category?

8. Does the Christian go back and forth from spiritual to carnal and carnal to spiritual? How often can this changing of categories take place?

9. When and how does a "carnal Christian" become a spiritual Christian?

10. Are there different degrees of carnality and different degrees of sanctification among so-called spiritual Christians?

If some of these questions seem a bit ridiculous, it is because they grow out of a ridiculous, unbiblical teaching. "Carnal Christian" teachers would not run into such questions if they studied carefully the following questions and answers from the Westminster Larger Catechism:

Q. 75. *What is sanctification?*

A. Sanctification is a work of God's grace, whereby they whom God hath, before the foundation of the world, chosen to be holy, are in time, through the powerful operation of his Spirit applying the death and resurrection of Christ unto them, renewed in their whole man after the image of God; having the seeds of repentance unto life, and all other saving graces, put into their hearts, and those graces so stirred up, increased, and strengthened, as that they more and more die unto sin, and rise unto newness of life. . . .

Q. 77. *Wherein do justification and sanctification differ?*

A. Although sanctification be inseparably joined with justification, yet they differ, in that God in justification imputeth the righteousness of Christ; in sanctification his Spirit infuseth grace, and enableth to the exercise thereof; in the former, sin is pardoned; in the other, it is subdued: the one doth equally free all believers from the revenging wrath of God, and that perfectly in this life, that they never fall into condemnation; the other is neither equal in all, nor in this life perfect in any, but growing up to perfection.

Q. 78. *Whence ariseth the imperfection of sanctification in believers?*

A. The imperfection of sanctification in believers ariseth from the remnants of sin abiding in every part of them, and the perpetual lustings of the flesh against the spirit; whereby they are often foiled with temptations, and fall into many sins, are hindered in all their spiritual services, and their best works are imperfect and defiled in the sight of God.

Reviewing the Problems in "Carnal Christian" Teaching

We have identified several significant problems and dangers with "carnal Christian" doctrine: (1) It is based on an erroneous interpretation of 1 Corinthians 3:1–4. (2) It corrupts many other doctrines of the Christian faith. (3) It separates the two main doctrines of the Christian faith—justification and sanctification and thereby separates the blessings of the new covenant. (4) It makes holiness, obedience, discipleship, and submission to Christ optional (compare John 10:26–28; 14:21–23; 15:10; Titus 2:10–14; Heb. 12:14; 1 Peter 1:15, 16). In addition, (5) the "carnal Christian" teaching breeds antinomianism and gives a false standard of what it means to be a Christian. (6) It is the mother of many of the second-work-of-grace errors. (7) It teaches two ways to heaven: the "carnal Christian" way and the spiritual Christian way—whichever you prefer. (8) It also ignores the biblical distinction between the ground of salvation and the grounds of assurance. (8) And it breeds a false spirituality or pharisaism in so-called "spiritual Christians" who have measured up to some man-made standard of spirituality.

There ought to be no professed "spiritual Christians," much less "super-spiritual" ones! George Whitefield, a man who lived in very close communion with his Savior, prayed all his days, "Let me begin to be a Christian." Another saint has expressed it well: "In the life of the most perfect Christian there is every day renewed occasion for self-abhorrence, for repentance, for renewed application to the blood of Christ, for application of the rekindling of the Holy Spirit."

Many are comfortable living sinful lives while hiding behind a teaching that is not biblical—comfortably going to hell on a false teaching. It is one thing to acknowledge that Christians have carnal outbreaks. It is another thing altogether to teach that someone whose life is predominantly carnal should be considered a Christian.

From the human vantage point the visible church is made up of professors and possessors. But from the divine perspective it is made up only of genuine possessors of salvation. Since we are on the human side, we should take note of three truths from Matthew 3:12, where John the Baptist says of our Lord, "His winnowing fan is in His hand, and He will thoroughly purge His threshing floor, and gather His wheat into the barn; but He will burn up the chaff with unquenchable fire." The three truths are these:

1. There will be a separation of the real from the spurious, the true from the false, the possessors from professors.
2. The time of this separation is not now.
3. The winnowing fan in not in our hands.

We do not always know who has been born again. Therefore, when speaking of the backslider, two errors must be avoided: (1) insisting that he is *not* a Christian; (2) insisting that he *is* a Christian. We do not know, we cannot know. And it is not a sin not to know.

That is just what makes the "carnal Christian" doctrine so dangerous, so deceiving, and so damning. How do you know the backslider's profession was genuine or not? You don't! If such a person gives no evidence of being born again, there are always two possibilities: he may be a true Christian in a backslidden condition, or he may never have been savingly united to Christ. Only God knows, which is why we should not offer false assurances to people who show no signs of spiritual life. We would do better to say "I don't know" than to squeeze out of Scripture a category that the Holy Spirit never put there—the "carnal Christian."

A Closer Look at 1 Corinthians 2:14–4:15

Let us consider more closely the single passage on which the "carnal Christian" teaching is based, 1 Corinthians 2:14–4:15. The words of one of the church fathers are very appropriate to our examination of this text: "If you only have one Scripture on which to base an important doctrine or teaching, you are most likely to find, on close examination, that you have none." This is precisely what we have with the theory that divides humanity into three categories.

As I have stated, the primary purpose of 1 Corinthians was not to lay a doctrinal foundation (despite this letter's wealth of theology) but to deal with practical problems in a young church less than a century old. The portion of Scripture we are considering deals in particular with one of the many problems in the church at Corinth, namely schism between Christians over various ministers, as the following verses indicate:

- "For it has been declared to me concerning you, my brethren, by those of Chloe's household, that there are contentions among you. Now I say this, that each of you says, 'I am of Paul,' or 'I am of Apollos,' or 'I am of Cephas,' or 'I am of Christ'" (1 Cor. 1:11–12).
- "For when one says, 'I am of Paul,' and another, 'I am of Apollos,' are you not carnal? Who then is Paul, and who is Apollos, but ministers through whom you believed, as the Lord gave to each one? I planted, Apollos watered, but God gave the increase" (1 Cor. 3:4–6).
- "Therefore let no one glory in men. For all things are yours: whether Paul or Apollos or Cephas, or the

world or life or death, or things present or things to come—all are yours. And you are Christ's, and Christ is God's" (1 Cor. 3:21–23).

- "Let a man so consider us, as servants of Christ and stewards of the mysteries of God. . . . Now these things, brethren, I have figuratively transferred to myself and Apollos for your sakes, that you may learn in us not to think beyond what is written, that none of you may be puffed up on behalf of one against the other" (1 Cor. 4:1, 6).

First Corinthians 2:14–4:15 deals principally with one problem—schism. And this problem, like all the other problems addressed in 1 Corinthians (such as defrauding one another, disorder at the Lord's Table, etc.) resulted from carnality, the principle of remaining sin in all believers. Paul describes the same principle in Romans 7:21–23: "I find then a law, that evil is present with me, the one who wills to do good. For I delight in the law of God according to the inward man. But I see another law in my members, warring against the law of my mind, and bringing me into captivity to the law of sin which is in my members."

In chapter 1 the Corinthians had gotten off to a good start. Paul says that they were sanctified in Christ Jesus (v. 2); they were recipients of the grace of God (v. 4); they were enriched by Christ in all utterance and knowledge (v. 5); the testimony of Christ was confirmed in them (v. 6); and they came short in no gifts (v. 7).

But some of the Corinthian Christians attached themselves to one great Christian teacher or another, thus setting up rival parties. Some followed Paul, some admired Apollos, and others extolled Peter.

Instead of saying, "We are Christ's disciples," and uniting together in Him, they developed factions and expressed attitudes that said: "We are Paul's, he founded the church." Or, "Apollos is more eloquent than the apostle, and he edifies us more; we have gone beyond Paul, therefore, we are of Apollos." Or, "We are of Peter." They were making idols out of these mere men, who were only co-laborers in God's vineyard. This was causing "envying, strife and division" (3:3). Acting like the unregenerate in their factions over the different servants of Christ, they were carnal in that area of their lives.

Paul charges them with carnality and puts their divisions into a biblical perspective.

- Their ministers were only ministers (v. 5).
- All these ministers carried on the same design and purpose (vv. 6–10).
- The ministers were building on the same foundation (vv. 11–15).
- The people should not have gloried in particular ministers because they should have had an equal interest in all true ministers. "All are yours. And you are Christ's" (vv. 22–23).

First Corinthians 3 resumes Paul's discussion of contentions introduced in 1:11–13. Chapter 3 makes a transition from Paul's defense of his preaching (see chap. 2) to the subject of divisions (3:1–5) and the relationship of ministers to the church as servants, not party leaders. In verses 5–20 Paul sets forth several key observations concerning the ministerial office:

- Ministers are servants without any authority or power of their own. One may plant, another may water, *but only God can give the increase* (vv. 5–7).
- Ministers are one. They have one Master, one work, but different functions in that great work. They are like fellow laborers on the same farm or fellow builders of the same temple (vv. 8–9).
- In discharging their duty they have a great responsibility as to how they build and what they build—the church of God (vv. 10–15).

95

- Because the church of God is the temple of God, ministers will be held accountable for the doctrine they teach and preach in executing their duties (vv. 16–17).
- No minister should deceive himself. He cannot preach a higher wisdom than the wisdom of God, and to learn that wisdom he must renounce his own (vv. 18–20).

The apostle is not setting up three categories of men. He knows only two classes—natural and spiritual. Under the term "natural" Paul includes all those who are not partakers of the Spirit of God. "But the natural man does not receive the things of the Spirit of God, for they are foolishness to him; nor can he know them, because they are spiritually discerned" (1 Cor. 2:14). If the Spirit of God has not given them a new and higher nature than they ever possessed by their natural birth, they are natural men.

Those who are spiritual may be but babes in grace and in knowledge. Their faith may be weak. Their love may be in its early bud. Their spiritual senses may be little exercised. Their faults may be in excess of their virtues. But if the root of the matter is in them, they have passed from death unto life, passed out of the region of nature into what is beyond nature—the state of grace. Paul puts them in another class—all of them. They are spiritual men. The difference is that the spiritual receive the things of the Spirit, embrace them with delight and feed upon them with intense satisfaction.

In 1 Corinthians 2:14–16 there is no third category of people characterized by carnality in every area of their lives. Yes, there is growth in grace and knowledge; and there are Christians with many degrees of carnality. But the Bible does not teach three categories of men. Scripture knows only two final destinies, heaven and hell; two ways, the narrow way that leads to life and the broad way that leads to destruction; two principles that govern a person's walk, the Spirit principle and the flesh principle. First Corinthians 3:1–4 is not expounding a general truth about categories of men but reproving a specific outbreak of carnal behavior. If we want to be true to Scripture, we must not misinterpret this text by accommodating it to the miserable performance or inordinate affections of men.

Paul's Teaching on 1 Corinthians 3:10–15

Few passages of Scripture have been subjected to more numerous and more contradictory explanations than 1 Corinthians 3:10–15. Though in 1 Corinthians 2 Paul is defending his apostleship, the whole context from 1 Corinthians 2:1 to 4:15 has to do with ministers and how they are meant to build the church. In 3:7 Paul makes it very clear that the success of the gospel is not produced by preachers or teachers themselves—they are mere instruments—"but God gives the increase." Though in 3:10 and 4:15 Paul points out that he did the most important work on the human side—he laid the foundation—he is quick to warn his readers, "Let no one glory in men . . ." (3:21).

According to verse 10, Paul was used of God to be a "wise master builder." Since he was the last apostle, others coming after him would have a lesser rank (Eph. 4:11). There are no more apostles. The church has been built on the once-for-all "foundation of the apostles and prophets, Jesus Christ Himself being the chief cornerstone" (Eph. 2:20). Ministers, teachers, and church leaders, building upon that foundation of divine revelation, set forth the fundamental doctrines of Scriptures, which center on Christ crucified for our salvation (1 Pet. 2:6; Matt. 21:42).

Throughout 1 Corinthians 3, the words "every man" and "any man" (KJV) or "each one" and "anyone" (NKJV) refer to ministers, who build the church through their roles of teaching and preaching. The focus is on "each one's work" (v. 13), "anyone's work" (v. 14). And it is crucial for us to see that there are two kinds of work, corresponding to two kinds of material used. The character of each minister's work "will become manifest" on the Day of Judgment, when "it will be revealed by fire," for "the fire will test each one's work, of what sort it is" (v. 13). Works built with gold, silver, and precious stones will stand the final test. Works using the materials wood, hay, and stubble will not stand the test (vv. 12–15; see also Matt. 3:12; 7:24–27; 13:24–30).

These two kinds of materials (gold, silver, and precious stones versus wood, hay, and stubble) represent two different classes of church members—true and false professors of faith. One class is proved by fire to be genuine and the other is not. We see the same principle in the parable of the wheat and the tares (Matt. 13:24–30), in the analogy of the two foundations—one sand, the other rock (Matt. 7:24–27), and in the parable of the ten virgins—half of whom were real and the other half spurious (Matt. 25:1–12).

Two things should be clear from our study of 1 Corinthians 3:10–15.

First, Paul is emphasizing the unity among true believers in the church. The church rests on one sure foundation held together by Jesus Christ. Strife and contention over various ministers is out of character with the unity believers have as "God's husbandry" (v. 9, KJV) and "the temple of God" (v. 16). The church is one, grounded in the truth of Christ.

Second, within the one church are two groups, but they are not spiritual versus "carnal" Christians. They are those who will be manifest by fire to be genuine Christians and those who will be manifest to be false. The gold, silver, and precious stones are true, regenerate believers, the results of the labors of wise and faithful ministers. The wood, hay, and stubble represent spurious converts, unconverted professors of religion introduced into the church by less judicious laborers. On the Day of Judgment the church universal will be tested by the holy, searching, and penetrating inquest of God the Judge, even as a material building is tested when a torch is applied to it. The living Rock on which the church is founded and the imperishable stones and precious metals will remain after the conflagration, but the perishable materials would be utterly consumed.

Nominal Christians—spurious converts, whose faith is a dead faith, however affiliated they may be with an orthodox church of Christ—will be cast into hell and forever consumed by God's wrath, while true Christians will remain uninjured. Ministers who by their soundness, prudence, and fidelity have added genuine converts to Christ's church will receive a reward from the free grace of their Lord. These ransomed souls, having stood the test of the Judgment Day, will shine as stars in their crowns. But this gracious reward will be lost by those injudicious and rash ministers who have introduced unsound professors into the church. If the ministers are themselves built on the Rock, Christ Jesus, they will indeed be saved; but they will see the unregenerate members whom they have brought into God's house sink to hell under His strict judgment and will wear in heaven a crown stripped of its jewels. (I strongly recommend Robert L. Dabney's comments on 1 Cor. 3:10–15 in *Dabney's Discussions* [reprint, London: Banner of Truth, 1967], 1:1:551ff.)

Implications for Evangelism

Our study of these momentous truths ought to result in more true evangelism. The "carnal Christian" teaching is, after all, the consequence of a shallow, man-centered evangelism in which decisions are sought at any price and with any methods.

When those pronounced to be converts do not act like Christians, do not love what Christians love or hate what Christians hate, and do not willingly serve Christ in His church, some explanation must be found other than calling them "carnal Christians" and asking them to make yet another decision. They have already done that and have already been declared, by a preacher or group leader, to be "Christians." But still, something is terribly wrong.

The teaching I have sought to expose says that the trouble is that they are just "carnal Christians"; they have not made Christ "Lord" of their lives; they have not let Him occupy the throne of their hearts. This unscriptural explanation is closely connected with faulty methods of evangelism. Too often modern evangelism has substituted an empty "decision" in the place of repentance and saving faith. Forgiveness is preached without an equal emphasis on a change of heart. As a result, decisions are mistaken as conversions even though there is no evidence of a supernatural work of God in a person's life.

Surely the best way to end this evil is to pray and labor for the restoration of New Testament evangelism! In such evangelism people will learn that it is not enough to profess faith, not enough to call Jesus "Lord, Lord" (Luke 6:46). The gospel preached in awakening power will summon men not to rest without biblical evidence that they are born of God. It will disturb those who, without good reason, have believed that they are already Christians. It will arouse backsliders by telling them that as long as they remain in that condition, they may never be genuine believers at all. And to understand this will bring new depths of compassion and urgency to the hearts of God's people in this fallen world.

One of the greatest hindrances to the recovery of such preaching is the theory we have considered. To reject that theory is to be brought back to a new starting point in evangelism and in the understanding of the Christian life. It is to bring God's work into the center of our thinking. It is to see afresh that there are only two alternatives—the natural life or the spiritual life, the broad way or the narrow way, the gospel "in word only" or the gospel "in power, and in the Holy Spirit" (1 Thess. 1:5), the house on the sand or the house on the rock.

There is no greater certainty than that an unchanged heart and a worldly life will bring a man to hell. "Let no one deceive you with empty words, for because of these things the wrath of God comes upon the sons of disobedience" (Eph. 5:6).

Not only in the world is evangelism needed. It is also needed in the church.

TEN

The "Carnal Christian" Teaching, 2— What Changes in Regeneration?

Another serious error related to the "carnal Christian" teaching of nonlordship theology is the two-nature theory—that the "new man" and the "old man" coexist in the believer. What we shall see is that the old-man–new-man teaching goes hand in hand with the idea of two classes of Christians—carnal and spiritual.

The Old and the New

As we saw in chapter 6, the nonlordship teaching on regeneration (the new birth) is that nothing in man's *nature* changes. The sinner's *standing*, which is his legal relationship to God, changes; but his *state,* that is, his condition on earth, does not necessarily change at the time of regeneration or even thereafter. The error of this teaching is not in its distinction between standing and state but in its denial that there is a vital connection between our standing and our state, that is, between justification and sanctification.

Thus this two-nature theory, like all theology, is interrelated to other doctrines. Once again we see how a person's views of justification and sanctification grow out of his view of regeneration.

One nonlordship leader summarizes regeneration this way:

> Regeneration is not a change of the old nature, but the introduction of a new. . . . Nor does the introduction of this new nature alter in the slightest degree the true, essential character of the old. This latter continues what it was, and is made in no respect better; yea, rather, there is a full display of its evil character in opposition of the new element.

This same nonlordship leader goes on to say: "It is a new birth, the imparting of a new life, the implantation of a new nature, the formation of a new man. The old nature remains in all its distinctness, and the new nature has its own desires, its own habits, its own tendencies, its own affection. All these are spiritual, heavenly, divine." He adds these dangerous words: "Be warned that the old nature is unchanged."

Notice that in this nonlordship teaching the Spirit regenerates and indwells the person, implanting a new nature in the soul, but the old, fallen nature remains untouched and unchanged. One entirely different new nature is placed alongside the old one. The regenerate person is made a partaker of the divine nature, but this divine nature is distinct from his own unchanged nature.

The result is two distinct, opposite, and irreconcilable natures in the Christian.

What Has Changed?

Writes one antinomian teacher, "The hope of transforming the old nature into holiness is as vain as the dream of a philosopher's stone, which was to change the dross of earth into gold." Another nonlordship teacher puts it this way: "Flesh is flesh, nor can it ever be made aught else but flesh. The Holy Ghost did not come down on the day of Pentecost to improve nature or to do away with the fact of incurable evil."

As the above quotations indicate, the old nature is not changed in regeneration or at any time thereafter. A new nature has been added, but the old sinful nature and the new nature exist within the same person at the same time, and yet poles apart. In this dualism there is an absolute and antithetical split between the finite, created, sinful, old nature and the infinite, uncreated, sinless, new divine nature. The result is an underlying schizophrenia in which the two natures are never reconciled. The two eventually go their separate ways—the old nature ultimately to destruction (annihilation), and the new nature to eternal life.

How does this relate to the "carnal Christian"? The "carnal Christian" is one in whom the old nature is dominant. The spiritual Christian is one who, for some reason, is controlled by the indwelling divine nature. We can only wonder how the spiritual nature gains dominance over a supposedly unchanged carnal nature. In the nonlordship teaching the evil nature is not at all weakened by grace, but rather inflamed. The old nature remains in all its distinctness, even as the new nature is introduced in all its distinctness. The new nature has its own desires, its own habits, its own tendencies, its own affections, all of which are spiritual, heavenly, divine. All the aspirations of the new nature are upward.

Thus this dualistic conflict between the two natures in each person underlies the nonlordship belief in two kinds of Christians—the spiritual and the carnal. The difference between them is whether the new nature or the old has gained control. It is not a matter of the old nature being made new. In nonlordship teaching, the old nature never changes. And the new nature cannot be justified or sanctified because it is the very nature of God Himself.

The nonlordship view of two utterly distinct natures or two selves, which continue unchanged throughout the earthly life, has peculiar implications. Robert L. Dabney tells the story of an emperor of Germany who bitterly rebuked a great episcopal feudatory for his violences, so inconsistent with his sacred character. The lord bishop answered that he represented two men in one, being both clergyman and baron, and that the military acts complained of were done in his secular character as feudal baron. "Well, then," replied the emperor, "bethink thee how the clergyman will fare when the baron is being roasted for his rapine and murder."

One profound implication of this two-nature view concerns the doctrine of sanctification. Writes Lewis Sperry Chafer (*Systematic Theology*), ". . . the experience of sanctification is absolutely unrelated to our position in Christ" (7:279–84). It is obvious that Chafer does not believe that there is an inseparable relationship between justification and sanctification. That is why many nonlordship teachers do not believe in progressive sanctification. Many, if not all, who hold that view teach that progressive sanctification is not to be expected.

The Lordship View—One Nature, Two Principles

The lordship teaching is that a new foundation for action, a new disposition, is implanted in the old ego. The Christian is one person with two struggling principles, a struggle in which the new principle is destined to conquer the old.

Not one text in the New Testament teaches that regeneration is the implanting of a new nature beside a remaining old one, or that the renewed man has two conflicting natures. Paul talks of two hostile *principles* warring in one nature. "But I see another law in my members, warring against the law of my mind, and bringing me into captivity to the law of sin which is in my members" (Rom. 7:23); "For the flesh lusts against the Spirit, and the Spirit against the flesh; and these are contrary to one another, so that you do not do the things that you wish" (Gal. 5:17). In these verses the great apostle teaches that the renewed man (still one man and one nature) is imperfect, having two principles of volition and mixed motives, even in the same acts. Paul does not teach in these passages, or any other, that the renewed man becomes two men or has two natures. The lordship teaching is that there is one nature, originally wholly sinful, which by regeneration is transformed so that it becomes progressively holy, though imperfectly so in this life. (I highly recommend Thomas Boston's *Human Nature in its Fourfold State* [Carlisle, Pa.: Banner of Truth, 1989], in which Boston describes human nature in the state of innocence, the state of nature, the state of grace, and the eternal state.)

But what about Paul's reference to "the old man" and "the new man" in Ephesians 4:22–24? Does it support the two-nature view of the Christian? Dr. Dabney makes the following comment on this passage:

> Among the texts which seem to favor this dualistic view, none is claimed with more confidence than Eph. 4:22–24, which speaks of "putting off the old man," and "putting on the new man." We note this as a specimen of the manner in which Scripture is overstrained, and an example of the way in which it may be cleared of these extravagances. One can hardly deny that, in this well-known passage, it is the most natural interpretation to regard the putting off of the old as in order to putting on of the new; then the two are not coexistent, but successive. But more decisively; Who is the old man, and who is the new? The obvious parallel in 1 Cor. 15:22, 45-49, shows that the "old man" is Adam, and the "new man" is Christ. The statement which we have to expound, then, is substantially this: that believers have "put off" Adam in order to "put on" Christ. That is, they have severed their connection with the first federal head, in order to enter into a connection with the second federal head.

John Newton, the great preacher and hymn writer, describes the inward warfare in a poem:

THE INWARD WARFARE
Galatians 5:17

Strange and mysterious is my life,
What opposites I feel within!
A stable peace, a constant strife;
The rule of grace, the power of sin:
Too often I am captive led,
Yet daily triumph in my Head.

I prize the privilege of prayer,
But oh! what backwardness to pray!
Though on the Lord I cast my care,
I feel its burden every day;
I seek His will in all I do,
Yet find my own is working too.

I call the promises my own,
And prize them more than mines of gold.
Yet though their sweetness I have known,
They leave me unimpressed and cold:
One hour upon the truth I feed,
The next I knew not what I read.

I love the holy day of rest,
When Jesus meets His gathered saints:
Sweet day, of all the week the best!
For its return my spirit pants;
Yet often, through my unbelief
It proves a day of guilt and grief.

While on my Saviour I rely,
I know my foes shall lose their aim,
And therefore dare their power defy,
Assured of conquest through His name;
But soon my confidence is slain,
And all my fears return again.

Thus different powers within me strive,
And grace and sin by turns prevail;
I grieve, rejoice, decline, revive,
And victory hangs in doubtful scale:
But Jesus has His promise past,
That grace shall overcome at last.

The foundational error behind the two-nature theory and the "carnal Christian" theory of the nonlordship teaching is the denial of progressive sanctification. If nonlordship teachers had more respect for what the Holy Spirit taught our Christian fathers concerning sanctification, they would not embrace or propagate the two-nature or "carnal Christian" views. As a sample of the historic view, the three paragraphs below are from chapter 13 of the Baptist Confession of 1689, which is identical in substance to the same chapter in the Westminster Confession of Faith:

1. They who are united to Christ, effectually called, and regenerated, having a new heart and a new spirit created in them through the virtue of Christ's death and resurrection, are also farther sanctified, really and personally, through the same virtue, by his Word and Spirit dwelling in them; the dominion of the whole body of sin is destroyed, and the several lusts thereof are more and more weakened and mortified, and they more and more quickened and strengthened in all saving graces, to the practice of all true holiness, without which no man shall see the Lord.

2. This sanctification is throughout the whole man, yet imperfect in this life; there abideth still some remnants of corruption in every part, whence ariseth a continual and irreconcilable war; the flesh lusting against the Spirit, and the Spirit against the flesh.

3. In which war, although the remaining corruption for a time may much prevail, yet, through the continual supply of strength from the sanctifying

Spirit of Christ, the regenerate part doth overcome; and so the saints grow in grace, perfecting holiness in the fear of God, pressing after an heavenly life, in evangelical obedience to all the commands which Christ, as Head and King, in his Word hath prescribed to them.

These three paragraphs are worlds away from the nonlordship teaching. If they are biblical, the nonlordship teaching cannot be true.

(In this chapter I am indebted to Robert L. Dabney's *Discussions: Evangelical and Theological* [Carlisle, Pa.: Banner of Truth, 1891, 1982], 1:190ff. I would also recommend John H. Gerstner's *Wrongly Dividing the Word of Truth: A Critique of Dispensationalism* [Brentwood, Tenn.: Wolgemuth & Hyatt]. For a more exhaustive study on our subject, I recommend John Owen, *Works of John Owen,* vol. 6, *Temptation and Sin, Mortification of Sin, Indwelling Sin in Believers* [Edinburgh: Banner of Truth, 1980].)

ELEVEN

Assurance of Grace and Salvation

While I have been distinguishing the lordship and nonlordship positions, I fully recognize that there are differences among nonlordship advocates, as well as among those who hold the lordship position. On most of the doctrines I have addressed, however, I have found unanimity among the most respected nonlordship teachers. For an accurate description of their position, I have relied on *Balancing the Christian Life* and *So Great Salvation* by Charles C. Ryrie, *Absolutely Free!* by Zane C. Hodges, and *The Savior, Sin, and Salvation* by Robert P. Lightner. Three of these books are a rebuttal of the lordship position of John MacArthur in his book *The Gospel According to Jesus*. I have also used Lewis Sperry Chafer's *Systematic Theology* and the notes of the Scofield Reference Bible.

In this chapter I will address the nonlordship view of assurance as set forth particularly in Hodges's 232-page book, *Absolutely Free!* The sources I will use to define and clarify the lordship view are the Westminster Confession of Faith and the Baptist Confession of 1689, also called the Old London Confession of Faith, which is based on the Westminster Confession. (I also recommend Thomas Brooks's *Heaven on Earth* and William Guthrie's *The Christian's Great Interest*.)

One of the most serious errors of the nonlordship teaching is its doctrine of assurance. Zane Hodges offers the following view in *Absolutely Free!* ([Grand Rapids: Zondervan, 1989], p. 50):

> But how, indeed, is this assurance conveyed? The answer by now should be obvious. The same miracle-working Word which regenerates also imparts assurance to the heart that believes. Indeed, the two things are both simultaneous and inseparable.
>
> Or to put it another way, when a person believes, that person has assurance of life eternal. How could it be otherwise?

As we shall see, both Hodges and the historic confessions cannot be right. The question is, Which one is biblical? To answer that question, I want to show the importance of assurance, define this wonderful doctrine, show the difference between false assurance and true assurance, and highlight six truths that the Bible and the confession teach about this comforting article of faith.

The Importance of Assurance

Having a clear understanding of the biblical teaching of assurance is important for all evangelism and counseling. Otherwise, many poor souls are misled or deceived about their salvation. A discerning pastor or counselor can function as a spiritual surgeon, cutting away false assurance and exposing a person's need for a genuine work of the Spirit.

A well-grounded assurance is also important because it is related to joy, comfort, and Christian service. How can someone have the joy of salvation if he is not sure he is in possession of salvation itself? William Cunningham wrote, ". . . the prevailing practical disregard of the privileges and duty of having assurance is, to no inconsiderable extent, the cause and effect of the low state of vital religion among us."

110

Thus the doctrine of assurance is highly important for evangelism, counseling, and vital, joyful Christian living, which we shall see more fully as we examine the meaning and implications of assurance.

What Is Assurance?

The following four paragraphs on the assurance of salvation are from the Baptist Confession of 1689, chapter 18:

1. Although temporary believers, and other un-regenerate men, may vainly deceive themselves with false hopes and carnal presumptions [*in an unspiritual way they take it for granted*] that they are in the favour of God and in a state of salvation, such a hope on their part will perish [*die away*].[1] Yet those who truly believe in the Lord Jesus, and love Him in sincerity, and who endeavor to walk in all good conscience be-fore Him, may be certainly assured in this life that they are in the state of grace, and may rejoice in the hope of the glory of God.[2] And such a hope shall never make them ashamed.[3] [*It will never disappoint them or let them down, for God will bless them, hear their prayers, and finally take them to glory.*]
[1] Job 8.13–14. Matt 7.22–23. [2] I John 2:3; 3.14–15; 5.13. [3] Rom 5.2–5.

2. This assurance is not merely a conjectural per-suasion [*something supposed to be true on slender grounds*] nor even a probable persuasion based upon a fallible hope. It is an infallible assurance of faith[4] founded on the blood and righteousness of Christ re-vealed in the Gospel.[5] [*It is based on a historical act of the Saviour of the world.*] It is also founded upon the inward evidence of those graces of the Spirit [*marks or evidences of grace*] in connection with definite promises made in the Scriptures,[6] and also on the tes-timony [*evidence*] of the Spirit of adoption Who wit-nesses with our spirits that we are the children of God

[*a felt, spiritual assurance*],[7] and Who uses the experience of assurance to keep our hearts both humble and holy.[8]

[4] Heb 6.11 & 19. [5] Heb 6.17–18. [6] 2 Pet 1.4–11. [7] Rom 8.15–16. [8] I John 3.1–3.

3. This infallible assurance is not so joined to the essence of faith that it is an automatic and inevitable experience. A true believer may wait long and fight with many difficulties before he becomes a partaker of it.[9] Yet, being enabled by the Spirit to know the things which are freely given to him by God, he may, without any extraordinary revelation attain this assurance by using the means of grace in the right way.[10]

Therefore it is the duty of every one to give the utmost diligence to make his calling and election sure, so that his heart may be enlarged in peace and joy in the Holy Spirit, in love and thankfulness to God, and in strength and cheerfulness for carrying out the duties of obedience. These duties are the natural fruits of assurance,[11] for it is far from inclining men to slackness.[12]

[9] Isa 50.10. Psa 88; 77.1–12. [10] I John 4.13. Heb 6.11–12. [11] Rom 5.1–5; 14.17. Psa 119.32. [12] Rom 6.1–2. Tit 2.11–14.

4. True believers may have the assurance of their salvation in various ways shaken, diminished, or intermitted [*suspended for a time*]. This may be because of their negligence in preserving it,[13] or by their falling into some special sin which wounds the conscience and grieves the Spirit,[14] or by some sudden or forceful temptation,[15] or by God's withdrawing the light of His countenance, and causing even those who fear Him to walk in darkness and to have no light.[16]

Yet, [*whatever the cause or duration of the impairment of assurance*] believers are never left without the seed of God [*essential spiritual identity*][17] and life of faith [*that hold on eternal values*],[18] that love of Christ and the brethren, that sincerity of heart and that conscience about their spiritual duty. Out of these things, by the operation of the Spirit, their assurance can in due time be revived,[19] and in the meantime the presence of these graces preserves them from utter despair.[20]

[13] Song 5.2–6. [14] Psa 51.8–14. [15] Psa 116.11; 77.708; 31.22. [16] Psa 30.7. [17] I John 3.9. [18] Luke 22.32. [19] Psa 42.5–11. [20] Lam 3.26–31.

Defined briefly, assurance is a God-given conviction of our standing in grace stamped on the mind and heart by the Spirit of God supernaturally. It is a conscious and experimental discerning of a saving relationship with God.

James Denny, the author of a classic volume on the atonement, *The Death of Christ*, said, "The acid test of any version of Christianity is its attitude toward assurance. Some regard it as a presumption; some regard it as a duty; the New Testament proclaims it as a fact." According to Thomas Goodwin, "Assurance is the 'White Stone' (Rev. 22:17) which none knows but he that receives it."

What specifically does the Bible teach us about assurance?

There Is a False Assurance

First, the Bible teaches that there is a false assurance in which unconverted men sometimes indulge, in which they are deceived, and in which they will finally be discovered. It is possible to place one's hope on insufficient grounds: "The hope of the hypocrite shall perish" (Job 8:13). Moreover, "The heart is deceitful . . ." (Jer. 17:9), and "if anyone thinks himself to be something, when he is nothing, he deceives himself" (Gal. 6:3). People are easily deceived in religious matters. The Pharisees were sure they were right with God and sought to evangelize others. Jesus warned them about false assurance: "Woe to you, scribes and Pharisees, hypocrites! For you travel land and sea to win one proselyte [convert], and when he is won, you make him twice as much a son of hell as yourselves" (Matt. 23:15).

It is because of the possibility of religious self-deception that we have the many warnings in the New Testament about spurious believers. The two houses in Matthew 7—one built on rock, the other on sand—both looked sound and true; but when the storm of God's judgment came, it was manifest that one was real and the other was not. The ten virgins in Matthew 25 all had the lamp of profession and assurance; but five were self-deceived, thinking they were saved and saying, "Lord, Lord," and Jesus had to say, "I do not know you" (v. 12). He will say the same thing to those who argue, "Lord, Lord, have we not prophesied in Your name, and cast out demons in Your name, and done many wonders in Your name?" (Matt. 7:22). They may have much assurance, but our Lord will say to them, "I never knew you; depart from Me, you who practice lawlessness!" The Bible teaches that there is a false assurance and gives many warnings against it.

There Is a True Assurance

Second, the Bible also teaches that there is a true assurance, in which believers are not deceived but rather confirmed, and in which they will not be confounded. This assurance rests upon (1) God's infallible Word, (2) the graces of which the Word speaks in the believer's heart, and (3) the testimony of the Spirit, which enables the believer to confirm the one by the other. "The Spirit Himself bears witness with our spirit that we are children of God" (Rom. 8:16). "We know that we have passed from death to life . . ." (1 John 3:14).

What Is the Difference?

Since there is a false assurance and a true assurance, a natural question is, What is the difference? A. A. Hodge, one of the outstanding theologians of the old Princeton Seminary, offers these distinctions in his chapter "Assurance of Grace and Salvation," in *Confession of Faith:* ([London: Banner of Truth, 1958], 239):

1. *True assurance* begets unfeigned humility.
   False assurance begets spiritual pride.
2. *True assurance* leads to increased diligence in the pursuit of holiness (Ps. 51:12–13, 19).
   False assurance leads to sloth and self-indulgence.
3. *True assurance* leads to candid self-examination and a desire to be searched and corrected by God: "Search me, O God, and know my heart: try me, and know my thoughts: And see if there be any wicked way in me, and lead me in the way everlasting" (Ps. 139:23–24, KJV).
   False assurance leads to a disposition to be satisfied with appearance and avoid accurate self-examination.
4. *True assurance* leads to constant aspiration after more intimate fellowship with God: "Beloved, now we are children of God; and it has not yet been revealed what we shall be, but we know that when He is revealed, we shall be like Him, for we shall see Him as He is. And everyone who has this hope in Him purifies himself, just as He is pure" (1 John 3:2–3).
   False assurance does not aspire after greater intimacy with God.

It is not the *strength* of one's convictions that proves the validity of his assurance, but the *character* of one's convictions.

A True Believer May Lack Assurance

Third, the Bible teaches that a true believer may lack assurance. The man in Mark 9:24 cried, "Lord, I believe; help my unbelief!" When he said, "I believe," he was *safe*, but when he said, "Help my unbelief!" it showed that he was *not sure*.

The distinction between faith and assurance is of great importance. It explains things that an inquirer sometimes finds hard to understand. Faith, let us remember, is the root, and assurance is the flower. Though you can never have the flower without the root, you can have the root without the flower.

Faith is that poor trembling woman, who came behind our Lord in the crowd and touched the hem of His garment.

Assurance is Stephen, standing calmly in the midst of his murderers, saying, "I see the heavens opened and the Son of Man standing at the right hand of God!" (Acts 7:56).

Faith is the penitent thief crying, "Lord, remember me" (Luke 23:42).

Assurance is Job sitting in the dust, covered with sores, saying, "I know that my Redeemer lives" (Job 19:25).

Faith is Peter's drowning cry as he began to sink, "Lord, save me!" (Matt. 14:30).

Assurance is that same Peter later declaring before the Sanhedrin, "There is no other name under heaven given among men by which we must be saved. . . . We cannot but speak the things which we have seen and heard" (Acts 4:12, 20).

Faith is Saul praying in the house of Judas at Damascus—sorrowful, blind, and alone.

Assurance is that same Paul, now an aged prisoner, calmly looking into the grave saying, "I know whom I have believed" (2 Tim. 1:12), and, "There is laid up for me a crown" (2 Tim. 4:8).

Faith is life. How great the blessing! Who can tell the great gulf between life and death? Yet life may be weak, sickly, painful, trying, worn, burdensome, joyless, to the last.

Assurance is more than life. It is health, strength, power, vigor, energy, comfort, and joy.

Faith is heaven by and by.

Assurance is heaven on earth.

Knowing the difference between faith and assurance is of crucial importance in counseling sinners, seekers, Christians, and backsliders.

Seek Assurance

Fourth, the Bible teaches that believers should seek to attain a well-grounded assurance.

- "Therefore, brethren, be even more diligent to make your calling and election sure, for if you do these things you will never stumble" (2 Peter 1:10).
- "And we desire that each one of you do show the same diligence to the full assurance of hope unto the end" (Heb. 6:11).

He who has such a hope can sing even in prison, as Paul and Silas did.

Assurance May Be Lost

Fifth, the Bible teaches that a true believer's assurance may be shaken, diminished, and intermitted because of negligence, sin, temptation, or trial. David lost his assurance, and in Psalm 51:12 he pleads for assurance to be restored: "Restore to me the joy of Your salvation, and uphold me with Your generous Spirit." Elsewhere he cries, "Lord, why do You cast off my soul? Why do You hide Your face from me?" (Ps. 88:14).

True believers may forfeit their assurance, and yet they are never entirely destitute of that seed of God. They therefore will not be left to sink into utter despair. Their assurance may in due time be revived by the operation of the Spirit.

Assurance Encourages Holiness

Sixth, the Bible teaches that assurance, instead of encouraging believers to indulge in sin, excites them to the pursuit of holiness. True biblical assurance cannot be attained or preserved without a close and blameless (not to imply perfectionism) walk with God according to His commandments and ordinances. "Beloved, now we are children of God; and it has not yet been revealed what we shall be, but we know that when He is revealed, we shall be like Him, for we shall see Him as He is. And everyone who has this hope in Him purifies himself, just as He is pure" (1 John 3:2–3).

117

The Ground of Salvation Versus
Grounds of Assurance

Before I show the differences between the lordship and non-lordship approaches to assurance, I want to make it clear that the ground of salvation and the grounds of assurance are two different things. Note that the following two questions have two different answers.

The first and the most important question anyone can ever seriously ask is, *What must I do to be saved?* There is only one biblical answer to this question: "Believe on the Lord Jesus Christ, and you will be saved"; or as the hymn writers have said, "My hope is built on nothing less than Jesus' blood and righteousness"; "Nothing in my hand I bring, simply to thy cross I cling."

The second question is, *How do I know that I have believed to the saving of my soul, that is, how do I know that my faith is saving faith?* This question has to do with assurance, and there are three answers—three elements or grounds of assurance. When speaking about the grounds of assurance, we need to be very clear that we are speaking of the ways a believer comes to true assurance, not the way a sinner comes to salvation or the ground on which salvation rests.

Three Grounds of Assurance

1. *The promises of God applied by the Spirit.* The first ground of assurance is the promises of God made alive by the Spirit of God. It is not just the promises of God alone. There must be the work of the Spirit in which the Spirit applies the Word by opening the sinner's understanding. The sinner has two problems. He needs sight because he is spiritually blind, and he needs light. The Bible is the light, a lamp to our feet. But light does not help blind people to see. They also need sight. For this reason I emphasize that the first ground of assurance is not only God's promises, but the promises of God made real by the Spirit of God.

This may be called "direct assurance," and this aspect of assurance is of the essence of faith. The principal acts of saving faith consist of accepting, receiving, and resting upon Christ alone for justification, sanctification, and eternal life, and it is impossible for someone to rest on Christ for salvation without believing or trusting that He will save him. Whoever rests on another person to do a certain thing must have a persuasion or assurance that he will in fact do it. This aspect of assurance is so essential to faith that without it, there can be no faith, human or divine. To believe a report is to be persuaded or assured of the truth of that report; to believe a promise is to be persuaded or assured that the promiser will do as he has said. In like manner, to believe in Christ for salvation is to be persuaded or assured that we shall be saved through the grace of our Lord Jesus Christ. Therefore, because of the nature of saving faith, this aspect of assurance is of the essence of faith. This direct element of assurance is the exercise of faith in Christ. It is an indispensable duty, which can never be superseded by any amount of evidences.

This direct exercise of faith in Christ is the unfailing source of relief and comfort in the Christian's darkest doubts. For in some dark and defeated hours the Christian will find nothing to assure him by looking inward or by looking for external evidences. We must look to Christ alone, the Son of righteousness, unchanged and unchangeable—still shining in all His glory behind whatever clouds may cast a dark and doubtful shadow on our souls.

Again, I want to emphasize, this ground of assurance is not just a promise intellectually grasped or memorized; it requires the illumination of the Spirit. There is no other cause that can make the promises of salvation effectual but the Spirit of God.

2. *The witness of the Spirit.* The second ground of assurance is the internal witness of the Holy Spirit. Paul tells us that "the Spirit Himself bears witness with our spirit that we

are children of God" (Rom. 8:16). And John says, "He who believes in the Son of God has the *witness* in himself (1 John 5:10). Here we have (1) the Christian described ("He who believes in the Son of God") and (2) internal satisfaction (assurance) experienced ("has the witness in himself").

The best of theologians differ in regard to the manner in which the Spirit gives this testimony. However, there is no disagreement that the witness of the Spirit is one of the grounds of assurance. The greater part of respected divines agree that the Spirit witnesses by means of His operations or the effect produced by Him in the hearts of believers. Rejecting the idea of an *immediate* testimony or some revelation apart from the Scriptures, they hold that the work of the Spirit is the testimony He gives believers, assuring them of their adoption and consequent safety.

Jonathan Edwards objects strongly to the view that the Spirit witnesses by way of immediate suggestion or revelation. He notes that many mischiefs have arisen from this false and delusive notion.

> What has misled many in their notion of that influence of the Spirit of God we are speaking of, is the word *witness*, its being called the witness of the Spirit. Hence they have taken it, not to be any effect or work of the Spirit upon the heart, giving evidence from whence men may argue that they are the children of God; but an inward immediate suggestion as though God inwardly spoke to the man, and testified to him, and told him that he was His child, by a kind of secret voice, or impression: not observing the manner in which the word *witness* or *testimony* is often used in the New Testament; where such terms often signify, not only a mere declaring and asserting a thing to be true, but holding forth evidence from whence a thing may be argued and proved to be true. Thus (Heb. 2:4), God is said to bear witness, with signs and wonders, and divers miracles and gifts of the Holy

Ghost. Now these miracles, here spoken of, are called God's witness, not because they are of the nature of assertions, but evidences and proofs. So also Acts 14:3; John 5:36; 10:25. So the water and the blood are said to bear witness (I John 5:8), not that they spake or asserted anything, but they were proofs and evidences. Indeed the apostle (in Rom. 8:16) speaks of the Spirit bearing witness with our spirit that we are the children of God, does sufficiently explain himself, if his words were but attended to. What is here expressed is connected with the two preceding verses, as resulting from what the apostle had there said, as every reader may see. The three verses together are thus: "For as many as are led by the Spirit of God, they are the sons of God; for ye have not received the Spirit of bondage again to fear; but ye have received the Spirit of adoption, whereby we cry, Abba Father: the Spirit Himself beareth witness with our spirit that we are the children of God." Here what the apostle says, if we take it together, plainly shows that what he has respect to, when he speaks of the Spirit's giving us witness or evidence that we are God's children, is his dwelling in us, and leading us, as a spirit of adoption, or spirit of a child, disposing us to behave towards God as to a Father.

This witness of the Spirit to the sonship of believers must never be divorced from the other activities of the Spirit in the sanctification of believers. The Spirit opens their minds to understand the Scriptures. The Spirit unveils to them more and more of the glory of Christ. And the Spirit sheds abroad in their hearts the love of God, thereby stirring up other holy affections and adorning them with the fruit of the Spirit.

3. *Christian character and conduct.* The third ground of assurance is Christian character and conduct, or assurance by evidence of regeneration or by the marks of grace. We could

call this "First John" assurance, for one cannot read that letter without seeing that Christian character and conduct have
something to do with assurance.

John is writing to believers to strengthen assurance. He
tells us that his purpose for writing 1 John is that believers
might *know* they have eternal life: "These things I have written to you who believe in the name of the Son of God, that
you may *know* that you have eternal life, and that you may
continue to believe in the name of the Son of God" (1 John
5:13).

Consider three questions about this verse: (1) To whom
is John writing? "To you who believe." (2) What is his purpose for writing? "That you may know . . ." (assurance). (3)
How are they to know? By "these things" which he has written in this letter. Notice that he is not going back to the gospel
of John. He wrote that gospel for a different reason, namely,
that men might believe and have life through Christ: "But
these are written that you may believe that Jesus is the Christ,
the Son of God, and that believing you may have life in His
name" (John 20:31).

What then are "these things" he has written in 1 John?
We might call them the "birth marks" of the second birth, or
"tests" of eternal life. "These things," these evidences of being born again, have a great deal to do with Christian character and conduct.

"Birth Marks" or "Tests" of Eternal Life

Let us look at some of the birth marks of the second birth,
or tests of eternal life.

1. *The test of belief.* "Whoever believes that Jesus is the
Christ is born of God . . ." (1 John 5:1). This birth mark includes the following:

- a belief in the Christ of the Bible as He is offered in
  the gospel—Prophet, Priest, and King of His church;

- a belief that reaches the whole man—his mind, affections, and will;
- a belief that has been revealed and applied by the Holy Spirit in regeneration;
- a belief acknowledged by the sinner in his response to the Savior;
- a belief that is apparent in the fruits of faith and repentance.

2. *The test of obedience.* "Now by this we do know that we know Him, if we keep His commandments. He who says, 'I know Him,' and does not keep His commandments, is a liar, and the truth is not in him. But whoever keeps His word, truly the love of God is perfected in him. By this we know that we are in Him" (1 John 2:3–5).

Bear in mind, John is not in this passage telling men how to become saved, or he would have told them what he wrote in his gospel: "Behold! The Lamb of God who takes away the sin of the world!" (John 1:29). In 1 John he is talking about knowing that we have eternal life (see 5:13), and he is saying that obedience has something to do with knowing we are born again.

3. *The test of love.* Love of the brethren is a birth mark of the second birth: "We know that we have passed from death to life, because we love the brethren" (1 John 3:14); "Everyone who loves is born of God and knows God" (1 John 4:7). Love of the brethren, therefore, is an important indication that we are born again.

4. *The test of doing righteousness.* ". . . you know that everyone that practices righteousness is born of Him" (1 John 2:29). Therefore, righteous living is an evidence of the new birth and has much to do with knowing we are born again, or having assurance.

There are other tests of eternal life in 1 John, but these are sufficient to make the point that Christian character and conduct have something to do with true biblical assurance and that the doctrine of assurance is vital in counseling sinners, seekers, those who profess faith, and backsliders.

Keeping the Grounds of Assurance Together

We have seen that there are three elements to a well-grounded assurance:

- The promises of God made real by the Spirit of God.
- The witness of the Spirit.
- Christian character and conduct.

Each of these three elements needs the other two in order for us to avoid distortion and false assurance. To hold exclusively to the first element of assurance, without the second and third, is *antinomianism,* the error of the nonlordship teaching. To hold exclusively to the second, without the first and third, is either *hypocrisy* or the *deepest self-deception or fantasy.* To hold exclusively to the third, without the first and second, is *legalism.*

Let me illustrate this by means of three questions that should concern every person who is serious about his own soul and about evangelizing others.

1. What is the only safe ground of a sinner's hope?
2. How does that only safe ground become the ground of my hope?
3. How am I to know that the only safe ground has become, and continues to be, the ground of my hope, so that I may be assured that my hope is not the "hope of the hypocrite" that shall perish, but the hope that "maketh not ashamed"?

Each question has its own answer, which must not be confused with the answer of either of the other questions.

1. The only safe ground of the sinner's hope is the sovereign mercy of God, exercised in accordance with His righteousness, through the atoning sacrifice of His Son, made known to us in the gospel revelation.
2. The only way in which this safe ground of hope can become the ground of my hope is by believing the Word of the truth of the gospel.
3. And the only way in which I can obtain permanent, satisfactory evidence that the only safe ground of hope has become the ground of my hope, is by continuing to believe the gospel, and by living under the influence of the gospel believed.

Counseling Seekers: Lordship and Nonlordship Approaches

There is a vast difference between the lordship and nonlordship approaches to counseling inquirers with regard to assurance. The nonlordship approach usually instructs the inquirer to find assurance along the lines of the following syllogism:

Major Premise:	He who believes in Christ is in the state of grace and shall be saved (John 3:16).
Minor Premise:	I believe in Christ.
Conclusion:	Therefore, I am saved; I have eternal life.

The syllogism is valid and the conclusion is true, provided the premises are true. And certainly the promise of God expressed in the major premise is true. But the question still remains, What about the minor premise? Do *I truly believe?* Or do I believe as did those our Lord described in John 2:23–24: "Now when He was in Jerusalem at the Passover, during the feast, many *believed* in His name when they saw the signs which He did. But Jesus did not commit Himself to them, because He knew all men"? They "believed" but were not saved; Jesus did not commit or entrust Himself to them.

Likewise, in John 12:42–43 Jesus tells us that many among the rulers "believed," but they would not confess Him. Surely they were not saved. Again, Jesus teaches that there are those who believe for a while, but in the time of temptation fall away: "The ones on the rock are those who, when they hear, receive the word with joy; and these have no root, who *believe for a while* and in time of temptation fall away" (Luke 8:13). They "believe" but are not saved.

Our syllogism, therefore, does not give us a full picture of biblical assurance. The syllogism illustrates that if we are not careful about our terms, we can reason our way into false conclusions—and false assurance.

The lordship view provides a fuller, undistorted picture of assurance by keeping in mind its three elements. For a well-grounded assurance, all elements are not only important but related to each other. In lordship evangelism the preacher or counselor never tries to do what only the Holy Spirit can do. The biblical view puts all preachers and evangelists out of the assurance business!

Let me illustrate the lordship approach, first from two passages in that immortal volume by John Bunyan, *Pilgrim's Progress* (Carlisle, Pa.: Banner of Truth, 1979), and then from the life and diary of a great missionary, David Brainerd.

In *Pilgrim's Progress* (pp. 3–4) Evangelist speaks to a seeking sinner under conviction:

> Evangelist [came] to him, and asked, Wherefore dost thou cry?
>
> He answered, Sir, I perceive by the Book in my hand, that I am condemned to die, and after that to come to Judgment; and I find that I am not willing to do the first, nor able to do the second.
>
> Then said, Evangelist, Why not willing to die, since this life is attended with so many evils? The man answered, Because I fear that this burden that is upon

my back, will sink me lower than the grave; and I shall fall into Tophet. And, Sir, if I be not fit to go to prison, I am not fit to go to Judgment, and from thence to execution; and the thoughts of these things make me cry.

Then said Evangelist, If this be thy condition, Why standest thou still? He answered, Because I know not whither to go. Then he gave him a Parchment Roll, and there was written within, Flee from the Wrath to come.

The Man therefore read it, and looking upon Evangelist very carefully, said, Whither must I flee? Then said Evangelist, pointing with his finger over a very wide field, Do you see yonder Wicket Gate? The man said, No: Then said the other, Do you see yonder Shining Light? He said, I think I do. Then said Evangelist, Keep that Light in your eye, and go directly thereto, so shalt thou see the Gate; at which, when thou knockest, it shall be told thee what thou shalt do.

Note several lessons from this example of lordship evangelism:

1. Evangelist does not give the seeker a three-step sales pitch, wring a decision out of him, and pronounce him saved by an oversimplified syllogism.
2. He points the seeker to the strait Gate and the narrow way.
3. He teaches him to follow the Light that God put on his path, so that he would get more light.
4. Evangelist does not try to play the Holy Spirit and give the seeker assurance.
5. Later Evangelist meets with him to give him additional instruction.

In the second example from *Pilgrim's Progress* (pp. 161–65), Hopeful has been converted through Faithful's testimony in Vanity Fair, where Faithful has been martyred. Long after Hopeful's conversion, when he and Christian were a bit weary on the way in a place called *enchanted ground,* they try to encourage each other by sharing their testimonies. The way Faithful dealt with Hopeful is a vivid lesson in personal evangelism and an illustration of the lordship principle that man should not try to do what only the Holy Spirit can do—give assurance.

We break in on this conversation between Christian and Hopeful. Hopeful has been telling Christian about the conviction of sin, and he begins to describe how Faithful dealt with him.

> *Chr.* And what did you do then?
>
> *Hope.* Do! I could not tell what to do, till I brake my mind to Faithful, for he and I were well acquainted. And he told me, that unless I could obtain the Righteousness of a man that never had sinned; neither mine own, nor all the Righteousness of the World could save me.
>
> *Chr.* And did you think he spake true?
>
> *Hope.* Had he told me so when I was pleased and satisfied with mine own amendments, I had called him Fool for his pains, but now, since I see mine own infirmity, and the Sin that cleaves to my best performance, I have been forced to be of his opinion.
>
> *Chr.* But did you think, when at first he suggested it to you, that there was such a man to be found, of whom it might justly be said, That he never committed Sin?
>
> *Hope.* I must confess the words at first sounded strangely, but after a little more talk and company with him, I had full conviction about it.
>
> *Chr.* And did you ask him, What man this was, and how you must be justified by him?
>
> *Hope.* Yes, and he told me it was the Lord Jesus that dwelleth on the right hand of the Most High: And

thus, said he you must be justified by him, even by trusting to what he hath done by himself in the days of his flesh, and suffered when he did hang on the Tree. I asked him further, how that Man's righteousness could be of that efficacy, as to justify another before God? And he told me, He was the Mighty God, and did what he did, and died the Death also, not for himself, but for me; to whom His doings, and the worthiness of them, should be imputed, if I believed on him.

Chr. And what did you do then?

Hope. I made my objections against my believing, for that I thought he was not willing to save me.

Chr. And what said Faithful to you then?

Hope. He bid me go to him and see; then I said it was Presumption; he said No, for I was Invited to come. Then he gave me a Book of Jesus his inditing, to encourage me the more freely to come; and he said concerning that Book, That every jot and tittle thereof stood firmer than Heaven and earth. Then I asked him what I must do when I came: And he told me, I must entreat upon my knees, with all my heart and soul, the Father to reveal him in me. Then I ask'd him further, how I must make my supplication to him? And he said, Go, and thou shalt find him upon a Mercy-Seat, where he sits all the year long, to give pardon and Forgiveness to them that come. I told him, that I knew not what to say when I came. And he bid me say to this effect:

God be merciful to me a Sinner, and make me to know and believe in Jesus Christ; for I see, that if his Righteousness had not been, or I have not Faith in that Righteousness, I am utterly cast away. Lord, I have heard that thou art a merciful God, and hast ordained that thy Son Jesus Christ should be the Savior of the World; and moreover, that thou art willing to bestow upon such a poor sinner as I am, (and I am a sinner indeed) Lord, take therefore this opportunity, and magnify thy Grace in the Salvation of my soul, through thy Son Jesus Christ. Amen.

Chr. And did you do as you were bidden?

Hope. Yes; over and over, and over.

Chr. And did the Father reveal his Son to you?

Hope. Not at the first, nor second, nor third, nor fourth, nor fifth; no, nor at the sixth time neither.

Chr. What did you do then?

Hope. What! why I could not tell what to do.

Chr. Had you not thoughts of leaving off praying?

Hope. Yes; an hundred times twice told.

Chr. And what was the reason you did not?

Hope. I believed that that was true, which had been told me, to wit, That without the Righteousness of this Christ, all the World could not save me; and therefore thought I with myself, if I leave off, I die, and I can but die at the Throne of Grace.

And withal this come into my mind, If it tarry, wait for it, because it will surely come, and will not tarry. So I continued Praying, until the Father shewed me his Son.

Chr. And how was he revealed to you?

Hope. I did not see him with my bodily eyes, but with the eyes of mine Understanding; and thus it was. One day I was very sad, I think sadder than at any one time of my life; and this sadness was through a fresh sight of the greatness and vileness of my Sins. And as I was then looking for nothing but hell, and the everlasting Damnation of my Soul, suddenly, as I thought, I saw the Lord Jesus looking down from heaven upon me, and saying, Believe on the Lord Jesus Christ, and thou shalt be saved.

But I replied, Lord I am a great, a very great Sinner: And he answered, My Grace is sufficient for thee. Then I said, but Lord, what is Believing. And then I saw from that saying [He that cometh to me shall never hunger, and he that believeth on me shall never

thirst] that Believing and Coming was all one; and
that he that came, that is, ran out in his heart and affection after Salvation by Christ, he indeed believed
in Christ. Then the water stood in mine eyes, and I
asked further, But Lord, may such a great Sinner as I
am, be indeed accepted of thee, and be saved by thee?
And I heard him say, and him that cometh to me, I
will in no wise cast out. Then I said, But how, Lord,
must I consider of thee in my coming to thee, that my
Faith may be placed aright upon thee. Then he said,
Christ Jesus came into the World to save Sinners. He
is the end of the Law for Righteousness to everyone
that believes. He died for our Sins, and rose again for
our Justification: He loved us, and washed us from
our Sins in his own blood: He is mediator between
God and us: he ever liveth to make Intercession for
us. From all which I gathered, that I must look for
Righteousness in his Person, and for Satisfaction for
my Sins by his Blood; that what he did in Obedience
to his Father's Law, and in submitting to the Penalty
thereof, was not for himself, but for him that will accept it for his Salvation, and be thankful. And now
was my heart full of joy, mine eyes full of tears, and
mine affections running over with love to the Name,
People, and Ways of Jesus Christ.

Chr. This was a Revelation of Christ to your soul
indeed; But tell me particularly what effect this had
upon your Spirit?

Hope. It made me see that all the World, notwithstanding in all the righteousness thereof, is in a state
of Condemnation. It made me see that God the Father, though he be just, can justify the coming Sinner:
It made me greatly ashamed of the Vileness of my former life, and confounded me with the sense of mine
own Ignorance; for there never came thought into my
heart before now, that showed me so the beauty of Jesus Christ: It made me love a Holy Life, and long to

do something for the honour and glory of the name of the Lord Jesus; Yea, I thought that had I now a thousand gallons of blood in my body, I could spill it all for the sake of the Lord Jesus.

Again, note that there is the absence of salesmanship or decisionism, and Faithful does not try to play the Holy Spirit by giving assurance.

We see this same principle in a passage from the life and diary of the great missionary David Brainerd (in *The Works of Jonathan Edwards*, 2 vols. [Edinburgh: Banner of Truth, 1974], 2:389):

July 2. Was obliged to leave these Indians at Cross-weksung, thinking it my duty, as soon as health would admit, again to visit those at the Forks of Delaware. When I came to take leave of them and spoke something particularly to each of them, they all earnestly inquired when I would come again, and expressed a great desire of being further instructed. And of their own accord agreed, that when I should come again, they would all meet and live together during my continuance with them; and that they would do their utmost endeavors to gather all the other Indians in these parts that were yet further remote. And when I parted, one told me with many tears, "She wished God would change her heart"; another, that "she wanted to find Christ"; and an old man that had been one of their chiefs, wept bitterly with concern for his soul. I then promised them to return as speedily as my health and business elsewhere would admit, and felt not a little concerned at parting, lest the good impressions then apparent upon numbers of them, might decline and wear off, when the means came to cease; and yet could not but hope that he who, I trusted, had begun a good work among them, and who I knew did not stand in need of means to carry it on, would maintain and promote it.

At the same time, I must confess that I had often seen encouraging appearances among the Indians elsewhere prove wholly abortive; and it appeared the favor would be so great, if God should now after I had passed through so considerable a series of almost fruitless labors and fatigues, and after my rising hopes had been so often frustrated among these poor pagans, give me any special success in my labors with them. I could not believe, and scarce dared to hope that the event would be so happy, scarce ever found myself more suspended between hope and fear, in any affair, or at any time, than this.

This encouraging disposition and readiness to receive instruction, now apparent among these Indians, seems to have been the happy effect of the conviction that one or two of them met with some time since at the Forks of Delaware, who have since endeavored to show their friends the evil of idolatry. And although the other Indians seemed but little to regard, but rather to deride them, yet this, perhaps, has put them into a thinking posture of mind, or at least, given them some thoughts about Christianity, and excited in some of them a curiosity to hear, and so made way for the present encouraging attention. An apprehension that this might be the case here, has given me encouragement that God may in such a manner bless the means I have used with Indians in other places, where there is as yet no appearance of it. If so, may His name have the glory of it; for I have learned by experience that he only can open the ear, engage the attention, and incline the heart of poor benighted, prejudiced pagans to receive instruction.

It cannot be overemphasized that anyone serious about biblical evangelism and counseling must study carefully what the Word of God teaches concerning assurance.

TWELVE

Self-Examination: Duties and Dangers

There are few subjects or exercises more neglected and yet more important to professing Christians than the subject of this chapter. This duty of self-examination may be called the lost doctrine of the Bible. It has been abandoned by the great body of professing Christians, including nonlordship teachers.

It is much easier to keep up external appearances or judge others than to scrutinize your own condition within. It is hard to read the tablet of one's own heart and to discover whether it is indeed a living epistle of Jesus Christ our Lord.

Self-examination is not only difficult but also potentially dangerous. Our true moral and spiritual state can be disclosed only by the Spirit and the Word. Since the final judge of the heart is God alone, the ultimate judgment belongs to the One whose eyes are like a flame of fire and who sees right through the deeds and thoughts of all creatures. The final word belongs to Him. And yet His revealed Word gives us guidance on how to perform the important duty of self-examination.

In the previous chapter we considered the biblical doctrine of assurance, which is so closely related to self-examination that perhaps the one should not be taught apart from the other. On the subject of this chapter, as with all the major doctrines we have been examining, the nonlordship teaching differs sharply with the lordship teaching. Few, if any, nonlordship teachers believe in self-examination at all.

The lordship teachers agree that, if not properly directed, self-examination can become morbid introspection. They emphasize that in carrying out this duty the Christian is meant to feel not the guilt of a condemning judge but the shame of an erring son. This duty poses no danger if we remember the comforting words of Romans 8:1: "There is therefore now no condemnation to those who are in Christ Jesus, who do not walk according to the flesh, but according to the Spirit."

That self-examination is a duty is clearly set out in many passages, such as Psalms 77:6; 139:23–24; 1 Corinthians 11:28–32; 2 Corinthians 13:5; and 2 Peter 1:10. For the purpose of this study we will confine ourselves to just two passages, 2 Corinthians 13:5 and 1 Corinthians 11:28–32.

2 Corinthians 13:5

Paul makes it very clear that self-examination is a duty when he writes: "Examine yourselves as to whether you are in the faith. Prove yourselves. Do you not know yourselves, that Jesus Christ is in you?—unless indeed you are disqualified" (2 Cor. 13:5).

Other versions translate this verse as follows:

- "Put yourselves to the proof, to see whether you are holding the Faith. Test yourselves. Surely you recognize this fact about yourselves—that Jesus Christ is in you! Unless indeed you cannot stand the test!" (TCNT).
- "You should be looking at yourselves to make sure that you are really Christ's. It is yourselves that you should be testing, not me. You ought to know by this time that Christ is in you, unless you are not real Christians at all" (PHILIPS).

136

The word translated "disqualified" in the NKJV is rendered "reprobates" in the KJV. Rather than meaning reprobate in a strict theological sense—that is, judicially abandoned to perdition—it means failing to pass the test, unapproved, counterfeit.

The two most common errors in managing the duty of self-examination are (1) examining by a false standard or a false conscience, and (2) examining in such a way that leads to morbid introspection. While we must discover our sin and guilt, this process should drive us to the gracious Sin-Bearer; not to despair, discouragement, or morbidity, but to fresh forgiveness, fresh assurance, joy, and peace. That is what the Lord's Supper is all about (which we shall see later).

Three things are very clear in this text:

1. Self-examination is a duty: "examine yourselves"; "prove yourselves."
2. The purpose of this duty is to know "whether you are in the faith."
3. The force of this duty is found in the words "unless indeed you are disqualified" or "except ye be reprobates" (KJV).

What Is Self-Examination?

First, self-examination is setting up court in your own conscience. This is a strange court because (1) you are the one on trial, (2) you are the lawyer presenting the case, and (3) you are the judge.

Second, self-examination is a spiritual inquisition.

Third, self-examination is an anatomy of the heart in which a person discloses the condition of his heart much as a watchmaker takes a watch apart to find defects.

Fourth, self-examination is a spiritual dialogue with yourself. It is not questioning the promises of God, as the nonlordship teachers would have us think, but rather questioning if we are among those to whom the promises are applicable. The proper exercise of this duty will keep us from coming under God's judgment. "If we would judge ourselves, we would not be judged" (1 Cor. 11:31).

In Jesus' parable in Matthew 22:12–13, He makes it clear that God will judge us as to whether we belong in His royal presence: "[The king] said to [one of the wedding guests], 'Friend, how did you come here without a wedding garment?' *And he was speechless.* Then said the king to the servants, 'Bind him hand and foot, take him away, and cast him into outer darkness; there will be weeping and gnashing of teeth.'"

The point is this: if you don't ask the questions, God will.

In spite of the clear command to "examine yourselves," the nonlordship teachers insist that self-examination leads to doubting God's promises and to morbid introspection. They tell us to look to God, not to ourselves. They say, "Just tell us about justification."

Surely, there is no more important doctrine in the Bible than justification by faith alone, and we are justified most freely by His grace alone, not any goodness we could find in ourselves. But the question must be asked, Who wants to be justified? Only those who see their need to be justified. And who wants forgiveness? Only those who sense their need of forgiveness. Though nonlordship teachers say, "Tell us about mercy, not self-examination," again we ask, Who wants mercy? Only those who see they are guilty. Where misery is not felt, mercy is not found.

Self-examination is like a title search in religion. Counterfeiters do not want their money examined. But imagine if everyone on the rolls of our churches would take this duty seriously and pursue it biblically.

1 Corinthians 11:28–32

That is what we are urged to do every time we take the Lord's Supper. Paul writes:

. . . let a man examine himself, and so let him eat of that bread and drink of that cup. For he who eats and drinks in an unworthy manner eats and drinks judgment to himself, not discerning the Lord's body. For this reason many are weak and sick among you, and many sleep. For if we could judge ourselves, we would not be judged. But when we are judged, we are chastened by the Lord, that we may not be condemned with the world." (1 Cor. 11:28–32)

This text teaches that self-examination is a preparatory command and is therefore very essential. The old Presbyterian church in my home town used to have what they called a "Preparatory Service" on the Friday night before the Sunday communion service. This preparatory service was meant to be a time not of morbid introspection but of discovering sin and guilt in order to come to the table for fresh forgiveness, joy, peace, and assurance that "Christ is mine and I am His."

Self-examination thus has a twofold purpose. It is meant not only to show us who is *not* a Christian, but also to show who *is* a Christian, and who therefore has all the benefits and blessings promised by God.

I once had a long-time friend and business associate whom I had every reason to believe was a true Christian; he was everything and did everything a Christian is meant to be and do. Yet sometimes he would go into deep depression and almost despair because he lacked assurance. He didn't understand self-examination, and thus he was robbed of comfort and assurance. He knew that Christ was sent to redeem men. He knew that a ransom had been paid on the cross for sinners. He knew that hell is avoidable. He knew that sin is pardonable and heaven is attainable. He knew that justification is freely offered. He also knew that it is all upon the condition of faith. But he did not know whether he had the kind of faith that entitled him to the promises and privileges of true believers. Proper self-examination solved his depressed state.

Why Is Self-Examination a Necessary Duty?

Self-examination is necessary for three reasons:

1. There is a difference between common grace and saving grace.
2. There is a difference between true faith and spurious faith.
3. Everyone reading these words is either in the state of grace or in the state of nature. That is, either you have been changed by the power of the gospel into the state of grace, or your nature is as it was when you came from your mother's womb.

Two families may be reading these words—the family of God, and the family of the Devil. You are in one or the other, for they are the two families that make up the entire world. Regardless of your blood relations or your outward affiliations, you need to examine yourself to know to which family you truly belong:

- There was a Cain in Adam's family.
- There was a Ham in Noah's ark.
- There was an Ishmael in Abraham's household.
- There was a Judas among our Savior's apostles.
- And at the Last Day the whole world will be divided into sheep and goats, those on the right hand and those on the left hand.

It is necessary to inquire whose we are. There is such a thing as having a right hope on insufficient grounds. "The hope of the hypocrite shall perish" (Job. 8:13).

This duty of self-examination requires diligence. That is why Peter said, "Therefore, brethren, be even more diligent to make your calling and election sure, for if you do these things you will never stumble" (2 Peter 1:10).

Have you ever asked yourself, Do I have the distinguishing traits of Christian character—not something I did in the past, but now? Can you answer that honestly? The self-deceived are in the most hazardous condition. When Jesus said, "Tax collectors and harlots enter the kingdom of God before you" (Matt. 21:31), to whom was He speaking? He was speaking to self-deceived religious people. Why? The harlot knew she was a harlot; the tax collector knew he was a tax collector. But the unconverted religious crowd was lost and did not know it. No one is at a greater disadvantage of obtaining true faith than those who have settled for a false faith.

Six Directives for Proper Self-Examination

Because of the dangers and perils associated with self-examination (its neglect and its abuse), let me offer six directives on how to perform this duty:

1. You must *know what the marks of a true Christian are,* that is, the distinguishing marks of a true Christian. He is not someone who is perfect. Nor is he someone who is indistinguishable from the world.

2. *Make the Word of God the rule or standard of your examination,* not the standards of men, churches, counsels, or conventions. The Bible is the standard of examination. For an honest look at yourself, it is necessary to take the candle of the God's Word into your soul. A Christian sins (1 John 1:8, 10) but does not sign a peace treaty with sin. Every little weed in your spiritual garden does not condemn you to perdition. The best of gardens have some weeds, though not so many as would choke off fruitful growth.

3. *Do not trust your heart's first reaction:* "He who trusts in his own heart is a fool" (Prov. 28:26). Your feelings may deceive you.

4. *Pray for the assistance of the Spirit.* The Word is a mirror. But a mirror in a dark room is useless. The Spirit is the light. (1) The Spirit gave the Word. (2) The Spirit is necessary to understand the Word. (3) The Spirit is necessary to apply

141

the Word. The Word and the Spirit work together, as mirror and light.

If you have the Word without the Spirit, you will dry up. If you have the Spirit without the Word, you will blow up. If you have the Spirit and the Word, you will grow up.

5. When you do find the marks of grace, *do not rest on the marks of grace for salvation.* We are not justified by our evidence. We may draw comfort from the evidence of our justification but must not have the least inclination of founding our hope on our marks or evidences. Marks and evidences are signs of our justification, not causes or instruments. Christ's righteousness only is our wedding garment. Liberty is a sign of the prisoner's pardon. But it was the Judge that set him free. His freedom is evidence of the court's action, not his own. Don't miss this point. Be sure, therefore, to distinguish between the *cause* of our justification and the *marks* or *evidences* by which it is made known.

6. *Don't come to conclusions about your relationship to Christ when it is wintertime in your soul.* Every true Christian knows of times when the heavens are brass. It is because of the wintertimes in our souls that self-examination is linked to the Lord's Table (1 Cor. 11:28). There we get a fresh start. A fresh view of ourselves will give us a fresh view of Christ, His love, and forgiveness of sin by His shed blood. The Lord's Supper was ordained because Christians still sin and still need to repent. The Christian life is one of lifelong repentance toward God and faith toward our Lord Jesus Christ. As we come to the Lord's Table, we make forgiveness fresh.

At the Table, Jesus is still for those who groan under the burden of sin. He is still the Great Physician. He is still the City of Refuge for the malefactor. He is still the Lifter-up of the downcast.

The duty of self-examination, if managed properly, keeps faith in Christ and repentance toward God fresh and vigorous. As A. A. Hodge has written: "True assurance leads to candid self-examination and to a desire to be searched and corrected by God. False assurance leads to a disposition to be satisfied with appearance and avoid accurate investigation" (*Confession of Faith* [London: Banner of Truth, 1958], 239).

Do You Pass the Exam?

There is no greater sign of a lack of saving faith than the neglect of self-examination. Paul said, "Examine yourselves as to whether you are in the faith" (2 Cor. 13:5). If you never do that, I believe I can draw from the text—"except ye be reprobates" (KJV)—that you are reprobate.

Do you pass the test? Do you feel the power and presence of Christ? Are you pretending something that is not real? Do you "have a name that you are alive, but you are dead" (Rev. 3:1)? (Though this passage refers to the church, it can also be applied to individuals.)

I do not wish to confuse anyone, and above all, I do not want to confuse those who have never professed to know Christ. I have been writing about the duty of self-examination for those who profess to be Christians, not about how to become a Christian.

Let me direct some words to you who make no profession of faith. You cannot go to heaven on your mother's religion, your father's religion, or your church membership. Therefore, I urge you to see Christ as your only hope. You need to be righteous before God, and you are not. This is where Christ enters the picture. Christ is our Righteousness. Come to Him.

A poem written by Robert Murray McCheyne sets forth Christ as our Righteousness:

JEHOVAH TSIDKENU—
THE LORD OUR RIGHTEOUSNESS

I once was a stranger to grace and to God,
I knew not my danger, and felt not my load;
Though friends spoke in rapture of Christ on the tree,
Jehovah Tsidkenu was nothing to me.

I oft read with pleasure to soothe or engage,
Isaiah's wild measure and John's simple page;
But e'en when they pictured the blood sprinkled tree,
Jehovah Tsidkenu seemed nothing to me.

Like tears from the daughters of Zion that roll,
I wept when the waters went over His soul;
Yet thought not that my sins had nailed to the tree,
Jehovah Tsidkenu—'twas nothing to me.

When free grace awoke me, by light from on high,
Then legal fears shook me, I trembled to die;
No refuge, no safety in self could I see . . .
Jehovah Tsidkenu my Saviour must be.

My terror all vanished before the sweet name;
My guilty fears banished, with boldness I came
To drink at the fountain, life-giving and free
Jehovah Tsidkenu is all things to me.

Jehovah Tsidkenu! My treasure and boast,
Jehovah Tsidkenu! I ne'er can be lost;
In thee I shall conquer by flood and by field
My cable, my anchor, my breastplate and shield.

Even treading the valley, the shadow of death,
This "watchword" shall rally my faltering breast
For when from life's fever my God sets me free,
Jehovah Tsidkenu my death-song shall be.

An Example of Self-Examination

The following is an example of how self-examination is prac-
ticed in the Christian Reformed Church, in preparation for
the Lord's Supper (from *The Psalter* [Grand Rapids: Eerdmans, 1927], 60):

That we may now celebrate the supper of the Lord to our comfort, it is necessary, before all things, rightly to examine ourselves; and further, to direct it to that end for which Christ has ordained and instituted the same—namely, to His remembrance.

The true examination of ourselves consists of these three parts:

First: Let every one consider by himself his sins and accursedness, that he may abhor himself and humble himself before God, considering that the wrath of God against sin is so great that He, rather than to leave it unpunished, has punished it in His beloved Son, Jesus Christ, with the bitter and shameful death of the cross.

Second: Let every one examine his heart whether he also believes this sure promise of God that all his sins are forgiven him only for the sake of the passion and death of Jesus Christ, and that the complete righteousness of Christ is imputed and freely given him as his own—yea, so completely as if he himself, in his own person, had satisfied for all his sins and fulfilled all righteousness.

Third: Let every one examine his conscience whether he is minded henceforth to show true thankfulness to God in his whole life, and so walk sincerely before His face; likewise, whether he, without any hypocrisy, heartily laying aside all enmity, hatred, and envy, earnestly resolves henceforward to live in true love and unity with his neighbor.

THIRTEEN

Good Works: The Fruits of Conversion

In this chapter we will consider the theological difference between nonlordship and lordship teachings on the relationship between faith and good works.

To be fair to the nonlordship position, let me quote from Zane C. Hodges. In his book *The Gospel Under Siege* (Dallas: Redencion Viva, 1981), Hodges writes that "there is no necessary connection between saving faith and works. In fact, to insist on good works as an evidence of salvation introduces obedience into the plan of salvation, compromising seriously, if not fatally, the freeness of the gospel offer" (p. 14). In other words, the nonlordship teaching sets up an antithesis between faith and works, rather than establishing the biblical connection and relationship between them. The nonlordship view does the same thing with law and grace, and with law and love—it sets up antitheses rather than showing the biblical harmony between them.

Salvation and Good Works

The power of God's grace to bring salvation through faith (Eph. 2:8) is the same power that produces good works through faith. That is because good works or sanctification is part of salvation, not something opposed to it. It is a serious mistake to think of salvation as stage one of the Christian life and sanctification as stage two. Salvation in the biblical sense encompasses all of God's saving work for and in His people—past, present, and future. As one Bible teacher used to emphasize, we *have been* saved (Eph. 2:8), we *are being* saved (1 Cor. 1:18), and we *shall be* saved (Rom. 13:11; 1 Peter 1:5). Salvation is not entrance into the Christian life; it is the whole Christian life, and good works and sanctification are an essential part of it.

So Paul says in 2 Thessalonians 2:13–14, "We are bound to give thanks to God always for you, brethren beloved by the Lord, because God from the beginning chose you *for salvation, through sanctification* by the Spirit and *belief in the truth*" (see also 1 Thess. 4:7–8; 1 Peter 1:2). Notice two things: First, we are not saved apart from sanctification. "God chose you *for salvation, through sanctification.*" It is an essential part of salvation, not an optional stage after conversion. Second, this process of salvation through sanctification happens "through . . . belief in the truth." That is, sanctification is by faith. Or to put it most plainly, the obedience that pleases God is the obedience of faith, and the obedience of faith is an essential part of salvation. We are chosen to be saved *through sanctification*, which is the same as good works and obedience of faith.

Martin Luther saw this clearly. Between October 1518 and October 1520 the indomitable Reformer had a two-year respite from the Roman siege. He worked feverishly, not knowing how long his safety would last. One of the works that came from this period was a little pamphlet called *The Freedom of a Christian.* Even in translation four centuries later, it vibrates with the passion of this ignited man. It captures (or should I say releases?) the connection between faith and holiness—between confidence in the promises of Christ and conformity to the person of Christ. Luther wrote:

It is a further function of faith that it honors him whom it trusts with the most reverent and highest regard, since it considers him truthful and trustworthy. . . . So when the soul firmly trusts God's promises, it regards him as truthful and righteous. . . . When this is done, the soul consents to his will. Then it hallows his name and allows itself to be treated according to God's good pleasure for, clinging to God's promises, it does not doubt that he who is true, just and wise will do, dispose, and provide all things well.

Is not such a soul most obedient to God in all things by this faith? What commandment is there that obedience has not completely fulfilled? . . . This obedience, however, is not rendered by works, but by faith alone.

We should never think of works as something unattached to saving faith as though the one could exist for long without the other. Obedience to Christ is the necessary result of true faith.

A statement on good works is beautifully set forth in the Westminster Confession of Faith, chapter 16 (quoted here), and the Baptist Confession of Faith of 1689.

I. Good works are only such as God hath commanded in his holy word, and not such as, without the warrant thereof, are devised by men, out of blind zeal, or upon any pretence of good intentions.

II. These good works, done in obedience to God's commandments, are the fruits and evidences of a true and lively faith: and by them believers manifest their thankfulness, strengthen their assurance, edify their brethren, adorn the profession of the gospel, stop the mouths of the adversaries, and glorify God, whose workmanship they are, created in Christ Jesus thereunto; that, having their fruit unto holiness, they may have the end, eternal life.

III. Their ability to do good works is not at all of themselves, but wholly from the Spirit of Christ. And that they may be enabled thereunto, besides the graces they have already received, there is required an actual influence of the same Holy Spirit to work in them to will and to do of his good pleasure: yet are they not hereupon to grow negligent, as if they were not bound to perform any duty unless upon a special motion of the Spirit; but they ought to be diligent in stirring up the graces of God that is in them.

IV. They who in their obedience attain to the greatest height which is possible in this life, are so far from being able to supererogate, and to do more than God requires, as that they fall short of much which in duty they are bound to do.

V. We cannot, by our best works, merit pardon of sin, or eternal life, at the hand of God, by reason of the great disproportion that is between them and the glory to come, and the infinite distance that is between us and God, whom by them we can neither profit nor satisfy for the debt of our former sins; but when we have done all we can, we have done but our duty, and are unprofitable servants; and because, as they are good they proceed from his Spirit; and as they are wrought by us they are defiled and mixed with so much weakness and imperfection, that they cannot endure the severity of God's judgment.

VI. Yet notwithstanding, the persons of believers being accepted through Christ, their good works also are accepted in him; not as though they were in this life wholly unblameable and unreproveable in God's sight; but that he, looking upon them in his Son, is pleased to accept and reward that which is sincere, although accompanied with many weaknesses and imperfections.

VII. Works done by unregenerate men, although, for the matter of them, they may be things which God commands, and of good use both to themselves and others; yet, because they proceed not from an heart purified by faith; nor are done in a right manner, according to the word; nor to a right end, the glory of God; they are therefore sinful, and cannot please God, nor make a man meet to receive grace from God. And yet their neglect of them is more sinful, and displeasing unto God.

Dr. Zacharais Ursinus, the principal author of the Heidelberg Catechism, is of great help to us on this subject of faith and works and their proper relationship to each other. Therefore, for the remainder of this chapter I will be drawing heavily from his *Commentary on the Heidelberg Catechism* (1852; reprint, Phillipsburg, N.J.: Presbyterian and Reformed, n.d.).

What Are Good Works?

For a work to be good and pleasing to God, three conditions are necessary:

1. It must be commanded by God. No creature has the right, or power, to institute the worship of God. The good works that I speak of are morally good and therefore are the same as the worship of God.
2. It must proceed from faith that rests upon the merit and intercession of Christ, from which faith we may know that we, together with our works, are acceptable to God for the sake of the Mediator. Speaking of this true faith the Scripture says, "Whatever is not from faith is sin" (Rom. 14:23), and "Without faith it is impossible to please [God]" (Heb. 11:6).
3. A good work must be intended principally for the honor and glory of God. Paul says, "Do all to the glory of God" (1 Cor. 10:31). In the words of Jesus, "Let your light so shine before men, that they may see your good works and glorify your Father in heaven" (Matt. 5:16).

Thus, good works are works that are performed according to the law of God, that proceed from true faith, and that are directed to the glory of God.

How May Good Works Be Performed?

Good works are possible only by the grace and assistance of the Holy Spirit operating within the regenerate alone. "Can the Ethiopian change his skin or the leopard its spots? Then may you also do good that are accustomed to do evil" (Jer. 13:23). ". . . neither can a corrupt tree bring forth good fruit" (Matt. 7:18, KJV). Without the righteousness of Christ imputed unto us, we are altogether unclean and abominable in the sight of God, and our works are as dung.

Are the Works of True Christians Perfectly Good?

Even the works of true Christian are never perfectly good, for at least three reasons: (1) Christians do many things that are evil in themselves, and they are guilty in the sight of God and deserve His righteous punishment. For example, Peter denied our blessed Lord three times; David committed adultery and murdered Uriah. Evil deeds may be called "sins of commission." (2) Christians omit doing many good things they ought to do. These failures may be called "sins of omission." (3) The good works that Christians perform are not so perfectly good and pure as God requires; for they are always marred with defects and polluted with sins. The greatest Christian that ever lived had to say, "I see another law in my members, warring against the law of my mind. . . . O wretched man that I am! Who will deliver me from this body of death? I thank God—through Jesus Christ our Lord . . ." (Rom. 7:23–25).

How Can a Christian's Imperfect Works Please God?

If a Christian's good works are always mixed with sin, how can they please God? There would be no purpose in performing them if they were not pleasing to God. How, then, do good works please Him? The answer is that good works are acceptable to God in Christ the Mediator, through faith—that is, on account of the merit and satisfaction of Christ imputed to us by faith and because of His intercession with the Father on our behalf.

Just as we in ourselves cannot please God, but only in His Son, so our works in themselves are acceptable to God only on account of the righteousness of Christ, which covers all our imperfection and impurity, so that it does not appear before God. As the Christian is acceptable on account of the Mediator, so his works are also pleasing to God for the sake of the Mediator. Therefore, the Christian and his works are covered by the perfect satisfaction of Christ. It is in view of this that Paul desires to "be found in Him, not having my own righteousness, which is from the law, but that which is through faith in Christ, the righteousness which is from God by faith" (Phil. 3:9).

Why Must the Christian Do Good Works?

There are three principal reasons why good works are to be performed by Christians: for the sake of God, on our own account, and for the good of our neighbor.

1. *Good works are to be done in respect to God.*

- Good works are to be done so that the glory of God our heavenly Father may be manifested: "Let your light so shine before men, that they may see your good works and glorify your Father in heaven" (Matt. 5:16).
- Good works are to be done so that we may render to God the obedience He requires. God requires the beginning of obedience in this life and the perfection of it in the life to come: "Having been set free from sin, you became the slaves of righteousness" (Rom. 6:18); "Present . . . your members as instruments of righteousness to God" (Rom. 6:13).

153

- Good works are to be done so that we may render to God the gratitude we owe Him. We declare our love and gratitude by our obedience and good works.

2. *Good works are to be done on our own account.*

- Good works are to be done so that by them we may testify of our faith and be assured of its sincerity by the fruits produced in our lives: "Every good tree bears good fruit" (Matt. 7:17); "[Be] filled with the fruits of righteousness which are by Jesus Christ, to the glory and praise of God" (Phil. 1:11); "Faith by it-self, if it does not have works, is dead" (James 2:17).
- Good works are to be done so that we may be assured that we have obtained the forgiveness of sin through Christ and that we are justified for His sake.
- Good works are to be done so that, by them, our faith may be exercised, nourished, strengthened, and increased.
- Good works are to be done so that we may adorn our profession, life, and calling: "I . . . beseech you to have a walk worthy of the calling with which you are called" (Eph. 4:1).
- Good works are to be done that we may escape temporal and eternal punishment: "Every tree that does not bear good fruit [works] is cut down and thrown into the fire" (Matt. 7:19).
- Good works must be done so that we may obtain from God those temporal and spiritual rewards which, according to the divine promise, accompany good works both in this life and the future life.

3. *Good works are to be done for the sake of our neighbor.*

- Good works are to be done so that we may be profitable to our neighbor and edify him by our example and deeds (see 2 Cor. 4:15).

- Good works are to be done that so we do not bring offense and scandal to the cause of Christ: "Woe to that man by whom the offense comes" (Matt. 18:7; see also Rom. 2:24).
- Good works must be done so that we may win the unbeliever to Christ: "And when you have returned to Me, strengthen your brethren" (Luke 22:32).

Summary

I know of no better way to summarize this study on good works than to quote question and answer 86 in the Heidelberg Catechism:

> Q. 86. Since then we are delivered from our misery, merely of grace through Christ, without any merit of ours, why must we still do good works?
>
> A. Because that Christ, having redeemed and delivered us by his blood, also renews us by his Holy Spirit, after his own image; that so we may testify, by the whole of our conduct, our gratitude to God for his blessings, and that he may be praised by us; also, that every one may be assured in himself of his faith, by the fruits thereof; and that by our godly conversation others may be gained to Christ.

This answer represents lordship teaching at its best. It is important to note that the catechism does not set up an antithesis between faith and works as the nonlordship teachers do in their writings. Rather, like the Bible, the catechism shows the relationship and connection between the two. Faith and works belong together; law and grace are true companions; law and love dwell as harmonious partners. Therefore, let us keep them joined together in the application of God's salvation. What God has joined together let no one put asunder.

FOURTEEN

The Law and the Gospel

In this chapter we come to what I consider to be the most serious theological difference between the nonlordship and lordship views, that is, their understandings of the relationship between the law (Ten Commandments) and the gospel.

The nonlordship and lordship teachings differ sharply in their answers to the following questions:

1. Does someone under grace have a duty to keep the Ten Commandments as a rule of life?
2. Does the gospel abrogate the Ten Commandments?
3. Does the law have a role in evangelism and the Christian life?

Most, if not all, nonlordship teachers deny that there is a necessary relationship or connection between law and grace. The moral law (Ten Commandments) to most nonlordship minds is nothing but the cold ashes of a burned-out, bygone religion.

Our Need for Moral Standards

The moral law carries permanent validity and goes straight to the root of our modern problems. It lays its finger on the church's deepest need in evangelism, as well as in the Christian life, sanctification. The Ten Commandments are desperately needed not only in the church but also in society. We live in a lawless age at the end of the twentieth century; lawlessness reigns in the home, in the church, in the school, and in the land. With a 25-percent illegitimacy rate and 56 percent of Americans saying in a recent survey that people who have babies out of wedlock should not be subject to moral reproach of any kind, most of the media makes light of virtues such as chastity and modesty. We are becoming worse than an immoral nation—we are becoming amoral. We are forsaking any fixed, objective standard of right and wrong.

Tragically, Christians have contributed to our society's moral decline by removing the Ten Commandments from their instruction, as nonlordship teachers have done.

The law restrains sin. Without the moral law this world would be a field of blood, as is evidenced in places where there is no regard for God's commands. The Puritan Samuel Bolton, in *The True Bounds of Christian Freedom* ([London: Banner of Truth, 1964], 79), said:

> Blessed be God that there is this fear upon the spirits of wicked men; otherwise we could not well live in the world. One man would be a devil to another. Every man would be a Cain to his brother, an Amon to his sister, an Absolom to his father, a Saul to himself, a Judas to his master; for what one does, all men would do, were it not for a restraint upon their spirits.

Not only the wicked, but also followers of God need an objective, fixed, yes absolute standard of right and wrong. A devotional life cannot exist without regard to morality. We cannot separate devotion from duty. After all, what constitutes a devout person? Someone who is seeking to do the will of God, someone who is instructed in sanctified behavior. And in what does sanctified behavior consist? In doing the will of God. And where do we find the will of God in respect to morality? In the only true standard summarizing the moral law—the Ten Commandments.

The Testimony of Three Witnesses

Consider the attitudes expressed by three of God's choice spokesmen regarding His law:

1. *David, a man after God's own heart—the sweet singer of Israel.*

- "Make me to go in the path of thy commandments; for therein do I delight" (Ps. 119:35, KJV).
- "Horror hath taken hold upon me because of the wicked that forsake thy law" (Ps. 119:53, KJV).
- "O how love I thy law! it is my meditation all the day" (Ps. 119:97, KJV).
- "I hate vain thoughts: but thy law do I love" (Ps. 119:113, KJV).
- "It is time for You to act, O Lord, for they have regarded Your law as void" (Ps. 119:126).

2. *Our Lord's chief apostle—Paul.*
- "Do we then make void the law through faith? Certainly not! On the contrary, we establish the law" (Rom. 3:31).
- "Therefore the law is holy, and the commandment holy and just and good" (Rom. 7:12).
- "For I delight in the law of God according to the inward man" (Rom. 7:22).
- "Therefore the law was our tutor to bring us to Christ, that we might be justified by faith" (Gal. 3:24).

3. *Our Lord Himself.*
- "Do not think that I came to destroy the Law or the Prophets. I did not come to destroy but to fulfill. For

assuredly, I say to you, till heaven and earth pass away, one jot or one tittle will by no means pass from the law till all is fulfilled" (Matt. 5:17–18).

We often hear the expression, "Be like Jesus." What was He like? He was perfect. How do we know? We must have a perfect standard by which to judge and that perfect standard is the perfect law of God (Ps. 19:7).

The Testimony of the Whole Bible

The importance of this subject is seen in that the whole Bible is either law or gospel—or law *and* gospel related. For example:

- The history of the Old and New Testaments, as far as man is concerned, is nothing more than narratives of lives lived in conformity or opposition to the moral law, or lived in belief or unbelief of the gospel.
- All the threatenings of the Old and New Testaments are threatenings either of the law or of the gospel. "He who believes in Him is not condemned; but he who does not believe is condemned already" (John 3:18). ". . . when the Lord Jesus is revealed from heaven with His mighty angels, in flaming fire taking vengeance on those who do not know God, and on those who do not obey the gospel of our Lord Jesus Christ. These shall be punished with everlasting destruction from the presence of the Lord and from the glory of His power" (2 Thess. 1:7–9).
- Every prophecy of Scripture is a declaration of things obscure and future and is connected with either law or gospel.
- Every promise is a promise related to either the law or the gospel, or both.
- Every admonition, reproof, or exhortation is with reference to the law or the gospel, or both.

160

Thus the law and the gospel are the center, the sum, and the substance of the whole Bible. How important then is it properly to relate and distinguish the two? The closer we get to a clear view of the difference between the law and the gospel, and the connection between them as they serve to establish each other, the more we will understand the Holy Scriptures and thus the will and mind of God, and the more useful we will be in His service.

Charles Spurgeon, in a sermon on Romans 5:20 (*New Park Street Pulpit,* sermon 37 [Grand Rapids: Zondervan], 1:286), declared:

> There is no point of biblical interpretation and application where men make greater mistakes than the relationship which exists between the Law and the Gospel. . . . some put Law instead of the Gospel; some modify the Law and the Gospel and therefore preach neither Law nor Gospel.
>
> If men blend the Law with the Gospel or Faith with Works (which is the same thing), especially in the area of Justification, they will obscure the glory of redeeming grace and prevent themselves and others from having the real joy and peace in believing. They will also retard their progress in holiness.
>
> Ah! but if men, under the influence of the Holy Spirit, are able to see the glory of the whole plan of Redemption—if they are able to reconcile the passages of Scripture which seem contrary to each other (and there are some) they would advance in true holiness and spiritual consolation.
>
> To see the glory of the whole would be a means to calm the conscience in times of mental and spiritual trouble. You see, a troubled conscience cannot be properly quieted unless the Gospel be rightly distinguished from the Law; on the other hand, there will be no troubled conscience to be quieted without the Law.

God's Character and Our Condition

Another indication of the importance of the law is that it reveals e two kinds of knowledge that are necessary for salvation:

1. *The law reveals the character of God.* God's law comes from His nature. The nature of God determines what is right, and the will of God imposes that standard upon all His creatures as a moral obligation. Since His will flows from His nature, and the law is perfect (Ps. 19:7), the law reflects the perfection of His nature.

Man is not answerable to an abstract law, but to God. Behind the law is the Lawgiver. Therefore, to find fault with the law is to find fault with the Lawgiver. The law is not the arbitrary edicts of a capricious despot, but the wise, holy, loving precepts of one who is jealous for His glory and for the good of His people.

Christ was perfect. How do we know? He kept the law perfectly—He was the law personified. Christ perfectly manifests the Father: "For in Him dwells all the fullness of the Godhead bodily" (Col. 2:9).

2. *The law reveals the condition of man.* To walk up to someone and say "All have sinned" does not bring conviction unless that person knows what sin is. "Sin is the transgression of the law" (1 John 3:4). "By the law is the knowledge of sin" (Rom. 3:20). The knowledge of sin as violation of God's law brings conviction.

The Law and Evangelism

Similarly, the importance of the law is seen in a subject that is dear to the heart of every true preacher and every true Christian—evangelism.

Let me quote several prominent saints to underscore the importance of the law in evangelism:

Luther.

The law must be laid upon those that are justified, that they may be shut up in the prison thereof, until the righteousness of faith comes—that, when they are cast down and humbled by the law, they should fly to Christ. The Lord humbles them, not to their destruction, but to their salvation. For God wounds, that he may heal again. He kills, that he may quicken again.

Augustine. "The conscience is not to be healed, if it is not wounded. Thou preachest and pressest the law, the judgment to come, with much earnestness and importunity. He which hears, if he is not terrified, if he is not troubled, is not to be comforted."

Tyndale. "It becomes the preacher of Christ's glad tidings, first through the opening of the law, to prove all things sin, that proceed not of the Spirit, and of faith in Christ; and thereby to bring him unto the knowledge of himself, and of his misery and wretchedness, that he might derive help."

Writing to John Firth, Tyndale says:

Expound the law truly, to condemn all flesh, and prove all men sinners, and all deeds under the law, (before mercy has taken away the condemnation thereof) to be sin, and damnable, and then as a faithful minister, set abroad the mercy of our Lord Jesus Christ, and let the wounded conscience drink of the water of life. And thus shall your preaching be with power, and not as hypocrites. And the Spirit of God shall work with you; and all consciences shall bear record unto you that it is so.

Beza. "Men are ever to be prepared for the gospel, by the preaching of the law."

Archbishop Ussher. "What order is there used in the delivery of the word, for the begetting of faith?" He answers:

> First, the covenant of the law is urged, to make sin, and the punishment thereof, known; whereupon the sting of conscience pricks the heart with a sense of God's wrath, and makes a man utterly to despair of any ability in himself to obtain everlasting life. After this preparation the promises of God are propounded; whereupon the sinner, conceiving a hope of pardon, looks to God for mercy.

Ezekiel Hopkins. "We find the same rules for our actions, the same duties required, the same sins forbidden in the Gospel as in the Law. The Law by which God rules us, is as dear to Him as the Gospel by which He saves us."

Charles Haddon Spurgeon (Metropolitan Tabernacle Pulpit, 30:15–16).

> The divine Spirit wounds before he heals, he kills before he makes alive. We usually draw a distinction between law-work and gospel-work; but law-work is the work of the Spirit of God, is so far a true gospel-work that it is a frequent preliminary to the joy and peace of the gospel. The law is the needle, which draws after it the silken thread of blessing, and you cannot get the thread into the stuff without the needle: men do not receive the liberty wherewith Christ makes them free till, first of all, they have felt bondage within their own spirit driving them to cry for liberty to the great Emancipator, the Lord Jesus Christ. This sense or spirit of bondage works for our salvation by leading us to cry for mercy.

John Calvin.

The true knowledge of God constrains us to worship Him, and that the true knowledge of self leads to genuine humility and self-abasement. The law is the instrument which the Lord uses to bring about both these results: by asserting therein His right to command, He calls us to pay Him the reverence due to His majesty; and by setting before us the standard of His righteousness, He shows us our unrighteousness and impotence. Moreover, the things which are taught in the tables of the law are also taught by that inward law which is written on the tables of every man's heart; for our conscience does not allow us to sleep an unbroken sleep, but inwardly testifies to us of the claims of God and of the difference between right and wrong. But since this inward law is insufficient, through our ignorance, pride, and self-love, God has given us also the plainer and surer testimony of the written law. From the law we learn that God, being our Creator, justly claims all that is due to a Father and a Master, namely, honor, reverence, love and fear: that we are not our own masters, at liberty to follow the desires of our own mind, without regard to His good pleasure: finally, that He loveth righteousness and hateth iniquity, and that we therefore must follow after righteousness in the whole course of our life unless we would be guilty of impious ingratitude to our Maker. Nor can we rightly excuse ourselves by alleging our inability to keep His law, seeing that the glory of God must not be measured by the extent of our powers, and that the sin which causes our inability lies within our own hearts and is righteously imputed to us alone.

John Bunyan. "The man who does not know the nature of the law cannot know the nature of sin. And he who does not know the nature of sin cannot know the nature of the Saviour."

In days gone by, children learned the commandments before they learned John 3:16, because only then did John 3:16 make any sense. Likewise, John Elliot's first translation work among the Indians was not of John 3:16 but of the Ten Commandments, and his first sermon was on the commandments. Did Elliot think the Indians would be saved by the Ten Commandments? Of course not, but the commandments would show them why they needed to be saved—they were law-breakers, and they needed a law-keeper to be their substitute.

John Paton, a great Presbyterian missionary to the New Hebrides, first taught the commandments. Why? People will never be properly interested in a relationship with the Redeemer until they see the terrible breach in their relationship to the Creator. The commandments are the moral mandate of the Creator to creatures. The sharp needle of the law makes way for the scarlet thread of the gospel. The law is indispensable in biblical, God-centered evangelism.

> Run and work the law commands
> but gives me neither feet nor hands.
> A sweeter sound the gospel brings;
> it bids me fly and gives me wings.

The Law and the Christian Life

Another indication of the importance of the law is its role in the Christian life. The law is a real standard for direction in the way of holiness. As such, it refutes every "second work of grace" teaching and rebukes spiritual pride in so-called spiritual Christians. The law makes Christians more grateful to Christ for fulfilling the commands for them and for enduring the curse in their place. It provides the only proper standard of sanctification, the only rule of obedience.

Nonlordship teachers may object, "But we have the Spirit." But to what moral conduct does the Spirit guide us? Paul answers that question in Romans 8:1–4:

There is therefore now no condemnation to those who are in Christ Jesus, who do not walk according to the flesh, but according to the Spirit. For the law of the Spirit of life in Christ Jesus has made me free from the law of sin and death. For what the law could not do in that it was weak through the flesh, God did by sending His own Son in the likeness of sinful flesh, on account of sin: He condemned sin in the flesh, that the righteous requirement of the law might be fulfilled in us who do not walk according to the flesh but according to the Spirit.

The Spirit guides us in a walk according to "the righteous requirement of the law." The Spirit writes the law on the heart.

A Summary of the Importance of the Law

1. The whole Bible is law and gospel, and the two are so vitally related to each other that an accurate knowledge of either cannot be obtained without the other.
2. The law reveals the character of God and the condition of man. These two kinds of knowledge are absolutely necessary for salvation. (See, for example, the first chapter in Calvin's *Institutes*.)
3. The law is essential to true biblical evangelism because by the law is the knowledge of sin. It was the law that was effective in Paul's conversion: "I would not have known sin except through the law" (Rom. 7:7).
4. The law is the only biblical rule and direction for obedience—that is, a sanctified life. In what does sanctified behavior consist? Doing the will of God. What is

167

the will of God in respect to morality? The moral law summarized in the Ten Commandments.

5. The law is one of three truths of the Bible that stand or fall together: the law, the Cross, and the righteous judgment of almighty God. (I will say more on this later.)

Law Versus Grace and Love?

The law tells us the right road to travel, but gives no strength for the journey. Because the Christian is under grace, he is enabled to do good. His being under grace never changes what is right or his need to obey God. The gospel frees us *to do* right, not *from doing* what is right—and the commandments are right. Echoing the fifth commandment, Paul says, "Children, obey your parents in the Lord, for this is right" (Eph. 6:1). Grace changes our relationship to what is right in this respect: it gives us power to do right. But grace never changes what is right. Nor does the gospel nullify the commands of God. The Great Commission (gospel) involves teaching all people to observe all of Jesus' commands (law) (Matt. 28:20).

The most insidious way to attack the moral law is to present it as antithetical to grace or the love of God. Some people seek to nullify the moral law by saying that it is replaced in the New Testament by the law of love. They fail to recognize that the law of love has always been connected with the commands of God, having been first given to Moses in Deuteronomy 6:5, shortly after the Ten Commandments in chapter 5. The law of love does not replace or nullify the commandments but summarizes them.

What is the love of God?

- "For this is the love of God, that we keep His commandments. And His commandments are not burdensome" (1 John 5:3).
- "Owe no one anything except to love one another, for he who loves another has fulfilled the law. For the commandments, 'You shall not commit adultery,'

'You shall not murder,' 'You shall not steal,' 'You shall not bear false witness,' 'You shall not covet,' and if there is any other commandment, are all summed up in this saying, namely, 'You shall love your neighbor as yourself.' Love does no harm to a neighbor; therefore love is the fulfillment of the law" (Rom. 13:8–10).

When Jesus summarized the law (Matt. 22:35–37; John 14:15, 21; 15:10), He taught us that the law is not our enemy, but sin is our enemy. Law and love are friends; law and grace are partners; law and liberty are companions; and the law and the Savior are soul mates.

Let me quote what I believe is one of the most important statements for any minister to grasp and put into practice, from Charles Bridges, *The Christian Ministry* (reprint, London: Banner of Truth,1958), 222:

The mark of a minister "approved unto God, a workman that needeth not to be ashamed," is, that he "rightly divide the word of truth." This implies a full and direct application of the gospel to the mass of his unconverted hearers, combined with a body of spiritual instruction to the several classes of Christians. His system will be marked by scriptural symmetry and comprehensiveness. It will embrace the whole revelation of God, in its doctrinal instructions, experimental privileges and practical results. This revelation is divided into two parts—the law and the gospel—essentially distinct from each other; though so intimately connected, that an accurate knowledge of either cannot be obtained without the other.

Our Need to Return to
Historic Teachings on God's Law

Declining ethical standards in our secularized society reflect a prevailing disregard for the moral law of God. The church is partly to blame for the moral decline seen in the home, school, work place, and society in general. Liberal theology has cut itself adrift from the importance of the Ten Commandments as they are given in the Bible. Nonlordship conservatives, despite their higher view of biblical authority, have also dispensed with the moral law as binding today. The need has never been greater for a return to the historic creeds for an appreciation of God's law and, with that, the lordship of Christ.

Let me quote from two of the most respected summaries of Christian doctrine ever written: first, Zacharias Ursinus's *Commentary on the Heidelberg Catechism* and, second, the Westminster Larger Catechism.

Ursinus on the Heidelberg Catechism. Almost 450 years ago Dr. Zacharais Ursinus was commissioned by the Elector Frederick of Heidelberg to write a catechism for systematic study of the doctrines presented in the Bible. He divided the Heidelberg Catechism into 52 lessons. Within the first three questions Ursinus asks, "Whence do you know your [sin and] misery?" The answer comes, "Out of the law of God."

Having shown, first of all, man's sinfulness from the law of God, Ursinus then sets forth how God sent His only begotten Son to be the Savior, who meets the demands of that law. Later in the catechism Ursinus explains that because Christ met the demands of the law for us, we stand in a new relationship to the law. It is now our standard by which we want to live in obedience before the God who has saved us.

In the introduction to his commentary on the Heidelberg Catechism, Ursinus discusses the topic, "What is the doctrine of the church?" His answer, quoted in part below, shows the true relationship of the law and the gospel, which is so neglected today and especially among nonlordship teachers.

> The doctrine of the church consists of two parts: the Law, and the Gospel; in which we have comprehended the sum and substance of the sacred Scriptures. The law is called the Decalogue, and the gospel

is the doctrine concerning Christ the mediator, and the free remission of sins, through faith. This division of the doctrine of the church is established by these plain and forcible arguments.

1. The whole doctrine comprised in the sacred writings, is either concerning the nature of God, his will, his works, or sin, which is the proper work of men and devils. But all these subjects are fully set forth and taught, either in the law, or in the gospel, or in both. Therefore, the law and gospel are the chief and general divisions of the holy scriptures, and comprise the entire doctrine comprehended therein.

2. Christ himself makes this division of the doctrine which he will have preached in his name, when he says, "Thus it is written, and thus it behoved Christ to suffer, and to rise from the dead the third day; and that repentance and remission of sins should be preached in his name." (Luke 24.46, 47.) But this embraces the entire substance of the law and gospel.

3. The writings of the prophets and apostles, comprise the old and new Testament, or covenant between God and man. It is, therefore, necessary that the principal parts of the covenant should be contained and explained in these writings, and that they should declare what God promises and grants unto us, viz: his favor, remission of sins, righteousness and eternal life; and also what he, in return, requires from us: which is faith and obedience. These, now, are the things which are taught in the law and gospel.

4. Christ is the substance and ground of the entire Scriptures. But the doctrine contained in the law and gospel is necessary to lead us to a knowledge of Christ and his benefits: for the law is our schoolmaster, to bring us to Christ, constraining us to fly to him, and showing us what that righteousness is, which he has wrought out, and now offers unto us. But the

171

gospel, professedly, treats of the person, office, and benefits of Christ. Therefore we have, in the law and gospel, the whole of the Scriptures, comprehending the doctrine revealed from heaven for our salvation.

Failing to see the harmony between law and grace, non-lordship preachers today proclaim a truncated gospel, resulting in rushed conversions and a shallow religious experience. That is why in the many years that I have spoken in churches or at conferences across the United States and abroad, I have sought to underscore the importance of the law of God as one of the three biblical truths that stand or fall together: (1) the law of God, (2) the cross of Christ, and (3) the righteous judgment of almighty God.

1. Do away with the law of God, and there is no sin because sin is the transgression of the law (see Rom. 3:20). First John 3:4 reads, "Whoever commits sin also commits lawlessness, and sin is lawlessness." No law, no sin. And if there is no sin, we need no Cross or Savior.

2. Without the work of Christ on the cross there is no solution for sin. In many respects one of the most wonderful descriptions of the work of Christ on the cross is found in Isaiah 42:21, which tell us, "He will magnify the law and make it honorable." The Cross without the law is a jigsaw puzzle with the key piece missing. The message of the Cross is Christ satisfying the righteous demands of a holy law. The base of the Cross is eternal justice, and the spirit of the Cross is eternal love. If there is no Cross, there is no gospel, and therefore no answer to the question of sin.

3. If there is no righteous judgment by almighty God, then who cares about sin or the Cross?

The Westminster Larger Catechism.

Q. 91. *What is the duty which God requireth of man?*
A. The duty which God requireth of man, is obedience to his revealed will.

Q. 92. *What did God at first reveal unto man as the rule of his obedience?*

A. The rule of obedience revealed to Adam in the estate of innocence, and to all mankind in him, besides a special command not to eat of the fruit of the tree of the knowledge of good and evil, was the moral law.

Q. 93. *What is the moral law?*

A. The moral law is the declaration of the will of God to mankind, directing and binding every one to personal, perfect, and perpetual conformity and obedience thereunto, in the frame and disposition of the whole man, soul and body, and in performance of all those duties of holiness and righteousness which he oweth to God and man: promising life upon the fulfilling, and threatening death upon the breach of it.

Q. 94. *Is there any use of the moral law to man since the fall?*

A. Although no man, since the fall, can attain to righteousness and life by the moral law; yet there is great use thereof, as well as common to all men, as peculiar either to the unregenerate, or the regenerate.

Q. 95. *Of what use is the moral law to all men?*

A. The moral law is of use to all men, to inform them of the holy nature and will of God, and of their duty, binding them to walk accordingly; to convince them of their disability to keep it, and of the sinful pollution of their nature, hearts, and lives: to humble them in the sense of their sin and misery, and thereby help them to a clearer sight of the need they have of Christ, and of the perfection of his obedience.

Q. 96. *What particular use is there of the moral law to unregenerate men?*

A. The moral law is of use to unregenerate men, to awaken their consciences to flee from wrath to come, and to drive them to Christ; or, upon their continuance in the estate and way of sin, to leave them inexcusable, and under the curse thereof.

Q. 97. What special use is there of the moral law to the regenerate?

A. Although they that are regenerate, and believe in Christ, be delivered from the moral law as a covenant of works, so as thereby they are neither justified nor condemned; yet, besides the general uses thereof common to them with all men, it is of special use, to show them how much they are bound to Christ for his fulfilling it, and enduring the curse thereof in their stead, and for their good; and thereby to provoke them to more thankfulness, and to express the same in their greater care to conform themselves thereunto as the rule of their obedience. . . .

Q. 99. What rules are to be observed for the right understanding of the ten commandments?

A. For the right understanding of the ten commandments, these rules are to be observed:

1. That the law is perfect, and bindeth every one to full conformity in the whole man unto the righteousness thereof, and unto entire obedience for ever; so as to require the utmost perfection of every duty, and to forbid the least degree of every sin.

2. That it is spiritual, and so reacheth the understanding, will, affections, and all other powers of the soul; as well as words, works, and gestures.

3. That one and the same thing, in divers respects, is required or forbidden in several commandments.

4. That as, where a duty is commanded, the contrary sin is forbidden; and, where a sin is forbidden, the contrary duty is commanded: so, where a promise is annexed, the contrary threatening is included; and, where a threatening is annexed, the contrary promise is included.

5. That what God forbids, is at no time to be done; what he commands, is always our duty; and yet every particular duty is not to be done at all times.

6. That under one sin or duty, all of the same kind are forbidden or commanded; together with all the causes, means, occasions, and appearances thereof, and provocations thereunto.

7. That what is forbidden or commanded to ourselves, we are bound, according to our places, to endeavor that it may be avoided or performed by others, according to the duty of their places.

8. That in what is commanded to others, we are bound, according to our places and callings, to be helpful to them; and to take heed of partaking with others in what is forbidden in them.

Epilogue

Little needs to be said in conclusion, except to stress the obvious and sacred importance that God in the Scripture attaches to the observance of His holy law. This must be taken to heart by every believer and preacher alike. The believer must increasingly delight in it "according to the inward man" (Rom. 7:22), demonstrating the truth of the Lord's saying, "If anyone loves Me, he will keep My word" (John 14:23). The preacher, likewise, must seek the help of the Holy Spirit to preach the gospel in a way that honors the law, and to expound the law in a way that sends men to the gospel. It brings no praise to God when either of these glorious ways is neglected.

As an aid to their hearers, preachers of the seventeenth and eighteenth centuries occasionally produced versifications of their sermons. These versifications could scarcely be called poetry, but their rhythm and rhyme greatly assisted in the retention of the truths contained in them. Ralph Erskine, a later Puritan from Scotland, produced a rhyme of this sort on the place of the law in the believer's life. Here is part of a sonnet of 386 verses that he entitles, "The Believer's Principles Concerning the Law and the Gospel."

> The law's a tutor much in vogue,
> To gospel-grace a pedagogue;
> The gospel to the law no less
> Than its full end for righteousness.
>
> When once the fiery law of God
> Has chas'd me to the gospel-road;
> Then back unto the holy law
> Most kindly gospel-grace will draw.
>
> When by the law to grace I'm schooled;
> Grace by the law will have me ruled;
> Hence, if I don't the law obey,
> I cannot keep the gospel-way.
>
> When I the gospel-news believe,
> Obedience to the law I give;
> And that both in its fed'ral dress,
> And as a rule of holiness.
>
> What in the gospel-mint is coined,
> The same is in the law enjoined:
> Whatever gospel-tidings teach,
> The law's authority doth reach.
>
> Here join the law and gospel hands,
> What this me teaches that commands:
> What virtuous forms the gospel please
> The same the law doth authorize.
>
> And thus the law-commandments seals
> Whatever gospel-grace reveals:
> The gospel also for my good
> Seals all the law-demands with blood.
>
> The law most perfect still remains,
> And every duty full contains:

The gospel its perfection speaks,
And therefore gives whate'er it seeks.

Law-threats and precepts both I see,
With gospel-promises agree;
They to the gospel are a fence,
And it to them a maintenance.

The law will justify all those
Who with the gospel-ransom close;
The gospel too approves for aye
All those that do the law obey.

A rigid master was the law
Demanding brick, denying straw;
But when with gospel-tongue it sings,
It bids me fly, and gives me wings.

In this paradox lies the perfect wisdom of God, and the appropriate prayer of the true believer may well be that of the psalmist, "Give me understanding, and I shall keep Your law; Indeed, I shall observe it with my whole heart" (Ps. 119:34).

Recommended Reading
on the Law

Bolton, Samuel. *True Bounds of Christian Freedom.* London: Banner of Truth, 1964.

Bonar, Horatius. *God's Way of Holiness.* Hertforshire: Evangelical Press, 1979.

Calvin, John. *Institutes of the Christian Religion.* Philadelphia: Westminster Press. Bk. 2, chaps. 7, 8, 11.

Chantry, Walter. *God's Righteous Kingdom.* Edinburgh: Banner of Truth, 1980.

Dagg, John L. *The Manual of Theology.* Harrisonburg Va.: Sprinkle, 1982. Pp. 233ff.

Fairbairn, Patrick. *The Revelation of the Law in Scripture.* Winona Lake, Ind.: 1979.

Kevan, Ernest. *The Grace of Law.* Grand Rapids: Baker, 1965.
———. *The Moral Law.* Escondido, Calif.: den Dulk, 1991.
Murray, John. *Principles of Conduct.* Grand Rapids: Eerdmans, 1957.
Ursinus, Zacharias. *Commentary on the Heidelberg Catechism.* Phillipsburg, N.J.: Presbyterian and Reformed. Pp. 489-618, especially 606ff.
The Westminster Larger Catechism. Qq. 93ff., especially 95–97, 99.